Whitewater Philosophy

Doug Ammons

*Wendy —
I hope you enjoy these
ideas & keep developing
your own. Best
Doug Leeds 3/16/09*

WNP
Water Nymph Press
Missoula, MT 59801
2009
www.dougammons.com

Front Cover Photograph copyright 2008 by John Salisbury

Ammons, Doug
Whitewater Philosophy/Doug Ammons
200 pages
ISBN: 0-9761580-1-9
   1.   Adventure. 2. Whitewater Kayaking. 3. Philosophy.
       4. Risk and Danger

PRINTED IN THE UNITED STATES OF AMERICA

Prepress work by Water Nymph Press
Printing by Quebecor Midland, Midland, MI

WNP
Water Nymph Press
415 Keith Ave.
Missoula, MT 59801
www.dougammons.com

Table of Contents

Introduction
Section 1: Basics   **Page**
Why I kayak   1
A Few Lessons in the Gray Zone   6
Beginner's Mind   11
A Different View of the River – Slalom Skills   16
The Bond of the River   21
Ode to the North Fork of the Payette   27
Paddler, Know Thyself   32
Niagara Falls and "Crazy"   37
The Real Shit: Why I Paddle Class V   44
The Lure of Numbers   54
The Meaning of Artificial Whitewater   63
Section 2: Bigger Issues
The Cutting Edge: A Beautiful Anarchy (Part 1)   68
      From Difficulty to Gifts (Part 2)   80
Soloing and taboos   93
Reflections on Danger and Certain Death   108
Making Sense of Death   113
Fear in Kayaking : Part 1   122
      Part 2: Psychology of Fear   135
      Part 3: Controlling Fear   151
Interview for www.SteepCreek.com   170
Section 3: Putting It All Together:
The Real Measure of Skill   186
Coyote Falls   201
Zanshin   210
The Voice of the River   216
Epilogue   219

Introduction

This book was not planned, but appeared in an unpredictable way out of my long time interest in flowing water and kayaking. For as long as I can remember, and certainly for my entire career as a whitewater kayaker, I've been drawn to those aspects of life that offered the greatest scope for change. I like adaptation and I like to be confronted with my limits, because only then is it possible to realize what holds me back and what I might be capable of. Kayaking is a sport ready-made to show those limits and demand change.

I began writing essays for myself over 20 years ago as a way to think through the experiences I had while kayaking. Flowing water is complex, and the closer I looked, the more lessons I learned. They ranged from the most immediate life and death disasters, to subtleties that defied description and challenged my understanding. Some ideas I've mulled over for many years, and I have thousands of pages of notes and hundreds of essays, articles, and ponderings at different stages of development. That number has only increased with time. The essays in this volume are just a few that I've put into final form – if there ever is such a thing as final.

I chose the word "philosophy" because every essay here is about our values and beliefs and expresses the ways in which the river becomes an intimate and important part of our lives. It is a rough-hewn but hopefully coherent set of themes about adventure sports, because all of them in their own ways confront us with the critical problem of how a weak, awkward human is able to fit into the natural world, and live with the sharp edges and awe-inspiring powers that pulse there. It doesn't matter whether one is dealing with water or air, snow or rock, in caves or high above the ground; our adventure sports form the modern Dao – they are ways of existing and expanding our awareness into the midst of the powers that shaped this astonishing planet.

The belief that prompts much of what I do is simple. It might be stated this way: all outward journeys should also be inward journeys. Without this, there is little personal change, still less meaning, and there certainly can be no philosophy. The outward journey is nothing without an equivalent journey within oneself; otherwise, we travel to the ends of the earth and yet stay exactly the same. I want something more than that.

In kayaking, as in other adventure sports, endless travel is trumpeted, striving for the highest, hardest, most stunning new descents, ascents, or feats. While I've done my share of this, I always had a nagging feeling as I watched the endless treadmill some of my friends and acquaintances walked, whether they were kayakers, climbers, extreme skiers, paragliders, or BASE jumpers. Trip after trip, gig after gig, video after video their travels across the globe played out, and yet some of them never seemed to change as people. They had an amazing wealth of experience and astonishing skills, and yet seemingly a poverty of making use of these things. The action of their sports seemed to function as an end in itself, almost as an escape rather than as a vehicle for something greater.

I don't mean to criticize these people, because I share many attitudes with them. Unquestionably, all are bright, engaging, skilled, and interesting. Many are my good friends. I only wish to say that personally I'm not interested in a path solely of action, without deeper reflection. Balanced, graceful action in the middle of chaos is a beautiful thing, enticing and compelling. You can marvel at it, like a miracle where the laws of entropy and chance have been repealed and astonishing feats somehow become possible. It is so compelling that it can uproot people and motivate them to a lifetime of paddling rivers or climbing mountains. This is a great experience, but not as an end in itself. Action is in many ways only the surface, and the most compelling truths do not lie on the surface of things.

Kayaking has left me with an undeniable thought: that adventure sports allow us to take part in the very powers that sculpted and shaped the world around us. That is a profound realization. It allows us a glimpse of the timelessness, change, and the infinite power of nature. When we move down a river, we are literally a part of the flow that scours the mountains and creates the vast landscape of continents. We can learn skills that allow us to join in the wordless wisdom of nature, but it is up to us to understand it, first to survive and then to respect and appreciate. The forces stir the beginner's joy in a simple surf, and sweep to a deep humility in the face of a massive, powerful rapid.

Because of where we go, all the adventure sports readily evolve into much more than sports. They aren't like baseball, soccer, or football. They don't have man-made rules. The rules are those of God and Nature, and of how the world is created. They aren't arbitrary or tweaked to make things fit humans, like the dimensions of the batter's box or the height of a basketball rim. They are life and death. They are how long you can hold your breath, how well you can hold your angle when the current slams on top of you, and how surely you can direct your path up or down a mountain, or through a raging rapid. These are elemental things, and no human law will ever have their power. They create a purity that draws certain kinds of people and not others. You have to be willing to stretch, to be thrown out of your comfort zone and adapt. It is not competition that is the draw, because there is no other team. The river or mountain is not your opponent. You do not fight it, even if the old stereotypes are of "conquering" Everest. So far as I can tell, Everest will still be there long after everybody who ever climbed it is dead. Tectonic movements will make it higher over the next ten million years, glaciers will tear away at its massive flanks and hurricane force winds will sweep its slopes every year, but humans will be no more. And the same simple thing is true of the rivers we run today and for the foreseeable future. There will be no sign of our passing, and no memory of our feats.

I don't believe in defining such places in terms of humans' games and limits. The more important view is that we attempt to learn to live within the greater powers and beauties of nature, and find wisdom there, truths about ourselves and our place in a larger world. I prefer looking at mountains and rivers and feeling their grandeur, rather than thinking in terms of racing to the top of a peak or down a rapid. The latter defines nature in human terms, the former confronts us with our human limitations in the face of much larger powers. Both can tell us something of what we are, but I find the greater depths lie in confronting ourselves with our weaknesses than in focusing on our supposed strengths. It is a simple truth that what we consider our greatest strengths are precisely our greatest weaknesses.

Rivers are just water, rocks and gravity, yet they produce the most astonishing beauty with a special kind of magic and infinite challenge. These create our sport and open the path to much more, including the path to changing ourselves. Stepping onto this path transforms the adventure sports into a very different venture. In particular, they become martial arts, where we live guided by a philosophy of both adventure and inner change instead of mere action. As the single greatest key: when ego is fed, vision is lost. When ego is cut through, insight is gained.

I've spent the last 25 years journeying through a world far more powerful than me, and this book is a small offering that describes a few things I've found along that path. Kayaking whitewater has deeply changed the way I look at the world, the skills I have, my judgment and perspective. The following essays deal with confronting limits and knowing ourselves, with risk, where fear comes from and how it can be overcome, with craziness, death and challenge, the real measure of skill, being alone, the bonds between partners, and much more. I have done my best to set down a few ideas, and I hope others will do more. For all the efforts we collectively have put into our adventures, so far we have very little philosophy to show for it. Most of what is there is piecemeal franticness, wry humor, tales of prowess, trashings, and dramatic stories of survival. Again, the focus is on action and not reflection, as if there are no other paths to follow. This is thin gruel and I reject it as an ultimate goal. It's fun, it's exciting, but it's not a goal. I would like to invite everybody to take a hand in developing a philosophy of adventure, starting with the sport and rivers we know so intimately. Living with one of the world's great powers puts us in a privileged position. We all feel that gift every time we put on a river, but it would be gratifying if we could be like the fabled alchemists of old, and transmute those feelings into a small number of clear truths.

There is much more to be done; I hope readers find a least a few ideas of interest and take them farther in ways I have not envisioned. When we start building instead of treating our sports like the beautiful anarchies they are, then perhaps we will see deeper into the world around us and especially, deeper into the worlds within us.

Acknowledgements:

Everybody I've ever been with on the river has contributed to this book and these ideas in some way. The full list would be very long, but I'd like to thank a few people in particular for prodding me over the years and for many valuable experiences: Rob Lesser, Bob McDougall, John Wasson, Charlie Munsey, Gerry Moffatt, Scott Lindgren, Monty Moravec, Risa Shimoda, Tommy Hilleke, Erik Boomer, John Salisbury, Ed Ward, Will Gadd, Brennan Guth, Corran Addison, Dave Manby, and Peter Knowles. Markus Schmid, Lukas Bluecher, Oli Grau, and Olaf Obsommer also have been inspirations.

Mike Kord has been a wonderful editor, sharp, insightful, and easy to work with. Ambrose Tuscano and Melissa Newell helped greatly with suggestions and discussions on many of the essays. Special thanks go to my close friend Jim Snyder, who for the past 15 years has served as a reliable and perceptive sounding board for many a crazy thought. Lastly, my wife Robin and our children have given me perspectives that run through every single idea here.

I am sincerely indebted to all these people.
Doug Ammons
Missoula, Montana.
February 2009

Section One: Basics

Why I Kayak

I am a kayaker, not a rafter. It is impossible to tell you the number of times people have made the mistake of calling my kayak a raft. While I respect all watercraft and I own four inflateables, people should realize the importance of the error. Although adventure, challenge, and fun can be had with any craft, kayaks are a special way to experience flowing water and rivers.

The crux of the distinction between kayaks and rafts is that kayakers carve deft, sharp lines down complex rapids. Our boats are sensitive to the smallest nudges of the water, and can slice through waves or edge like skis – a beautiful give and take with the river. They can fly off waterfalls and be twisted in the air, steered precisely or ricocheted, sliding like bobsleds down the polished rock of a steep creek, or cartwheeling in a wave like a graceful gymnast's body. All these qualities lead to what kayaking is and how we use it in our voyages down rivers, for fun and recreation, or much more serious endeavors. Simply put, rafts do not do these things.

The control involved in kayaking leads to a strong individualism. You alone are the pilot of your vessel and it obeys your commands – so long as your skills can handle what the river demands. On the other hand, rafts are for people who like a much simpler life with many more comforts and much more socializing. Rafts carry more than a kayak: both people and things like coolers, big tents, 16-ounce steaks and cast iron Dutch ovens. They are a more expansive view of life, like a motor home instead of a sports car. If rafts are full-bodied, then kayaks are minimalist. The two sports seem similar to outsiders, but they translate into very different river experiences.

Just like when people mistake kayaks for rafts, a similar problem is shown by the comment that kayakers are "looking for trouble" and emphasizing risk. That might be perfectly reasonable from some land-locked person's perspective. When hearing about some accident – a pin against a log, a broken leg going over a waterfall – somebody who leads a quiet life will ask a simple question: why do you kayak? What is the attraction of going out of your way to get killed? I understand that reaction. I've probably been asked those questions a thousand times, and I wrote a book that delves into the fun, excitement, thoughtfulness, and beauty of rivers. All the stories answer those questions. The fact is, no one goes out to look for trouble or get killed, and a single accident with one frightening miscalculation says very little about the other 99.99% of what we experience on rivers.

So you ask, what are those experiences? Well, kayaking has everything I've ever found enjoyable in music, sports, problem-solving, exploring, nature-loving, athletic challenge, and fun – all in a single activity. It's the best damn sport in the world.

Flowing water has all the qualities of music – infinite playfulness, subtlety of emotion, laughter, power, romping joy, mystery and depth. A kayaker uses his kayak, technique, and his understanding of the current to weave himself into a river. It is a graceful art and a hugely challenging sport. It's possible to find the entire range of human emotions in a trip down a river.

Water in any form, but especially moving water with all its force and intricacy, asks sharp questions and presents simple facts. A kayaker can readily find the river he is on to be both the master of Zen paradox and the clear eye of God. At its simplest and easiest, a river provides fun recreation and beautiful scenery – delightful experiences in a natural amusement park. At its most difficult, it demands you attain the highest levels of skill, ask life and death questions, and perform with complete commitment. If someone wants to address the physical manifestation of honesty, then they should kayak a difficult river. In ten minutes on a river I can learn more about what makes a person tick than in years of discussions. The pressure quickly brings out people's deepest feelings – whether they are confident, adaptable, brittle, or fearful. I enjoy cutting to the quick. I don't like bullshit. Kayaking suits me as a recreation and sympathetic life pursuit.

If you then add the exploration of new places, like first descent of remote rivers in a foreign country, then you open the doors even wider to physical hardship, cultural understanding, psychological and social stresses of all kinds – all with the simple and clear goal of getting down a river. In the end, this can become life itself within a beautiful and simplified purpose. Imagine physically moving through Beethoven's 9th symphony, or Bach's Passion, Handel's Messiah, or the best Rolling Stones' or Red Hot Chilli Peppers' concert - improvising with the force of the sound and emotion, immersing yourself in the power, aware of the tiniest nuances of structure and depth. That's the experience I get every time I do a trip down a challenging river. It is why twenty five years ago, I stopped my concert-level classical guitar playing and became a kayaker. When the kayaking bug really hit, as wonderful as Bach's music was, it wasn't a match for a crystal clear river cascading out of the mountains. Fortunately, ten years ago I started playing again because I realized that each kind of music has its place. I can't kayak the Stikine in my living room, but I can romp through a flamenco piece on my guitar.

Rivers are unbelievably rich pathways. They traverse altitude, time, culture, ecology, and geology. A trip in Nepal on the Thule Bheri took us from 14,000 feet near the Tibetan border, 250 kilometers to the Nepalese lowlands. We descended nearly 10,000 feet of whitewater, and rapid by rapid went from the high alpine valleys surrounded by 22,000 foot mountains, through every climatic zone down into the jungle. In 20 days, we went through a thousand years of civilization - from a medieval society of subsistence farming and herding, with no electricity, no phones, and no roads, to a roadhead with all of those, plus all the refuse brought by the clash of that medieval society with the 20th century. We went from a festival of shamanistic B'on Buddhism through a long cultural mixing zone, down into the heart of Hindu culture. Along the way, we ran some of the hardest whitewater ever done in such a remote venue up to that time. If treated with the proper respect, these are journeys with mind-shaking dimensions.

For most people, normal life is routine and predictable. Expeditions to hard rivers, particularly those in Third World countries, are full of open ended questions and problem solving, often in places where you don't even know the ground rules. Usually people live in the most comfortable cocoon they can construct, but that's not something I'm interested in. Stress is a great mirror. In my experience, people have all kinds of self-serving myths about themselves, but given enough stress it's possible to find the reality behind the myth. Personally, I find that process exciting, exhilarating – even if painful and sometimes really embarrassing.

Hard expeditions stretch people to their limits, physically and in their tolerance to cultural clash. Even the most energetic 25 year old can only miss so much sleep, get sick so many times, struggle through so many portages, eat so much freeze-dried food, and run so many rapids, before he reaches his limits. The unfamiliar bizarreness of other cultures wears you down bit by bit. Maybe the breaking point comes when you're trying to take a dump with 20 villagers watching you. Maybe it happens when you're just trying to find a little privacy after a long and difficult day on the river, but instead you have to change while surrounded by a few dozen curious people. They stare silently at you struggling out of soaking wet gear as you go hypothermic with the temperature at 20 degrees in a strong wind. Everybody reaches his or her limits in some way. Maybe to top things off you'll finish up by taking an exquisitely obnoxious 30-hour bus ride back to Kathmandu from the roadhead. Right when you're most exhausted, you're greeted by a nonstop assault on every sense – 30 hours of fingernails on chalkboards, shrill Hindu pop music wailing at 120 decibels, chickens crapping on your feet, people's elbows jammed into your ears, kicking you and your camera, screaming, exhaust, dust, rattling, checkpoints, and a raving psychotic drunk in the seat behind you. Maybe you end up knocking out the raving psychotic drunk with one punch.

In some form, there are wild stresses on every trip, whether to Africa, Mexico, Bolivia, or any other part of the third world. You can even find those limits during trips in the US and Canada with close friends. As obnoxious as they are at the time, after some rest and reflection you'll find they are touchstones about who you are. Over the years, weathering and then under-standing each weird incident has made me more effective in dealing with people and situations of all sorts. Plus I know how to clock a raving psychotic.

Rivers are educational in every sense. Preparing for a trip leads to studying the culture, religion, music, and everything regarding where you're going. I've met great people and made extremely good friends. These include my kayaking partners, who are among the very best people I've had the pleasure to know in this world. Others include experts on Mayan hiero-glyphs, B'on Buddhist monks, Hindu noblemen, Dutch ethno-musicologists, truck drivers, guitar makers, shaman, photo-graphers, adventurers, and just plain good people of all sorts.

Kayaking can be quiet meditation or intense excitement, thought-provoking adventure and passionate play. There is a wealth of opportunity for change, and the ability to incorporate a planet's life blood and pulse into your awareness.

Maybe more than everything else, I'm a kayaker because flowing water is soothing and comforting, and always resolves itself with the finality that only simple reality can. When you feel overwhelmed by the world, go to the nearest river. Find a quiet place and listen to the water. I have listened many times and my life is much richer for that.

It is possible to get these experiences in other ways, but for me, kayaking and flowing water have it all. So please don't call me a rafter and don't say I must be out there looking for trouble. Just give me a chance to tell you about the grandeur of rivers and why kayaking is the greatest sport in the world.

***

A Few Lessons in the Gray Zone

It's a good bet that we each remember the instant we got hooked on paddling. For one person, it might have been paddling a boat on a smooth lake, levitating across the water and feeling the freedom of a new world. For another, it was hurtling over that first horizonline into the rapid beyond. Regardless of when it took place, it was an instant of truth where we confronted something new and unknown. There was a rush – and for a moment we couldn't tell the difference between joy and the grab in our throat - but we knew without saying that it was a new path. And from that point on, nothing seemed the same.

To me, that instant holds the key to much of life's promise, because it encapsulates the single step where we move from what we know into the vast unknown. It may be the smallest step into the gray zone, but if we follow its different forms across our lives there are as many lessons as we could ever wish to learn.

If you've taught your children how to kayak or canoe it will carry you right back to the heart of that first experience. It will also remind you how much you now take for granted. Many years ago I took my oldest daughter kayaking for the first time down a river. She was about eight at the time, a natural athlete, strong, coordinated and almost fearless. Of course, she had paddled in pools, ponds, and lakes many times, and they had worked their magic on her. She was already hooked. But a river is very different place, even a little class I float like the Clark Fork River above Missoula.

We floated along in the current, bouncing through the little waves as the river cut gently between the cobble bars. Her pig tails flapped and she had a smile so big it hardly fit on her face. We saw two beavers and startled a Great Blue Heron along the bank. With a few ungainly strides he took wing and flapped slowly away downriver like a giant pterodactyl. There was no question that we had entered a magical world. The jolt came when impulsively she decided to get over to the side of the river. She forgot what we had practiced, forgot she was in a different realm and did what any good land-based thinker would do, quickly turned the boat and paddled straight for the side. At that moment without even realizing it, she entered the gray zone and came face to face with a profound fact: things are different out here. The upstream edge of her kayak caught and she almost flipped, the paddle spun out of her hand and the boat was swept downstream, barely staying upright. From fun to terror in zero seconds flat.

That's the problem and beauty of whitewater kayaking: more than any other sport, you can immediately find yourself in the gray zone without realizing you have crossed a line. Compare it with the safety and controlled environment of sport climbing. The step comes again, but in a different form. The first time I took her climbing was on a little sport route. Harness on, anchors set and checked, rope tied and checked, I had her climb up three feet, and then lean and test the rope. All fine, she laughed and swung around. "This is fun!"

I let out slack until she was back on the ground. It was only for an instant, then she whipped up the holds like an orangutan until about 20 feet off the deck she passed into the gray zone. She struggled with a move, slowed to a stop, and suddenly realized where she was. She froze and yelled, "It's too high!"

It was amazing to watch the beautiful, pure zen flow of movement collapse into paralysis and then a cry of, "I'm scared!"

Suddenly the minutia of physics became huge: "My foot's slipping!"

"It's okay," I calmed her, "Everything is okay. I have you here with the rope. You can just climb down."

"I can't! I'm going to fall!"

"No, I have you, remember we checked the rope, so just lean on it a little."

I snugged up the rope so it was tight and took most of her weight. "There, feel that?" She gingerly leaned, tested the rope, suspicious of whether it could be trusted, then eased off the holds. The rope stretched a little and she bounced gently. "Oh, it's a swing," she laughed and her confidence returned. Miraculous what a little security can do.

After talking her up to the top of the 40 foot cliff, I belayed her down. After a few breaths with both feet on the ground, she was pleased as punch, standing straight upright with her chest out, stating proudly, "I made it!"

"You were great, kid." I said. "You know, it's okay to be scared, just don't let it control you. Figure out what to do and do it." There were some very good lessons in that little climb.

The problem in kayaking is that the pace isn't yours to set. There isn't any rope to snug up or time to sit and think. Things can happen fast even on a slow river. The critical thing is, merely sitting in a kayak on water already has disconnected you from the solid things of the world. That happens the instant you push away from the bank and your world becomes fluid in every sense. You're on your own even when you're with dad.

Yet it is also amazing that kids learn how to play in that world in a matter of seconds. They can step blithely into the gray zone while adults fight against all those years of learning to be safe. Everything in the adult is screaming, "Watch out! You're going to get hurt!" while the kids are cool with it, because they haven't learned enough to worry. Their blessing is for uninhibited learning and the curse is being unaware of danger.

Another one of my daughters showed this. After watching me work with a friend she wanted to paddle. "Here, hold the paddle like this," I said.

She brushed me off, "I know."

"If you want to turn the boat, take strokes on the same side…"

"I know! Leave me alone."

I got out of the way and she paddled right off across the pool as if she'd been practicing for weeks, turning circles around the bemused college students. But when I took her out on the river for the first time, she had other worries. Everybody finds their own limits, the places where they wander into their own gray zones, and you can never guess ahead of time where that might be.

Sitting in the kayak with me hanging onto the cockpit, she peered over the side and looked suspiciously down into the water, "Are there fish down there?"

"Sure, they're looking for bugs to eat. Don't worry, I'm sure they're scared of you."

She ignored me and asked, "And snakes?"

"Well, maybe along the bank."

"That big rock scares me."

"It can't do anything to you. It's just sitting there on the bottom."

"I'm not going upside down in this river," she announced. "There are fish and snakes in it. And I don't like that big rock."

Sometimes, the gray we see hides the things we seek. But she learned to roll and loves being on the river, as she discovered the first time we headed off down the Blackfoot River. She saw the sun reflecting off all the little swirls of current around the rocks and shouted out, "Everything is moving! It's so beautiful!"

Joy and inspiration don't come from comfort. They come from the same place fear does – from confronting something different and larger than ourselves, and not knowing what will happen next. The steps come in a million forms. They happen in climbing, skiing, kayaking and they continue into our normal life. That is probably why adventure sports are so compelling. They present life in microcosm, simplified and elemental, symbolically carrying some of the biggest questions in a primal form. There's control and letting go; feeling safe and being scared, standing in the known and stepping into the unknown. We need faith in ourselves and the abilities of our children through all those lessons in the gray zone, both small and large – the trust that each of us will learn to live a full life, wherever that may lead.

***

Beginner's Mind

I'd like to offer you an idea from the martial arts that fits well within kayaking. I'm sure many of you have heard of it in one form or another. Importantly, it highlights some things that, although familiar in many ways, you may not have the words to describe. This is the idea of beginner's mind.

The term means many things, and our arena of moving water comes ready made to illustrate all of them. In Zen Buddhism it means an attitude of openness and eagerness, without preconceptions or judgment. It is a celebration of what is, rather than all the things that may come later. In martial arts, maybe the simplest meaning is that each time you step into the dojo you should be excited to learn, whether you are a white belt or a ninth degree black belt, and whether you are doing easy techniques you know well, or the most challenging moves you're capable of. Beginner's mind is a reminder to keep things fun, fresh, and new.

The idea can be applied in many ways to kayaking. Here are a few examples.

Years ago I stopped paying attention to water levels on most runs. It took half a career, but I realized that when you start describing a river by a number, it tells you certain things about the rapids or play spots, but like every label it hides more than it informs. I'd rather feel the river is alive and always more than any number we pin on it. If it's a difficult run where water level makes a serious difference, then the level is a good thing to know. But for anything less than that, I prefer to leave my mind open to what is actually there and not what I think should be there, or what I want to be there. This is the first step in finding something new. I am never disappointed, because there's always much that I've never seen before. It's all in how you look. If the essence of moving water is endless change, then the last thing I want to do is look at rivers in a static way.

Beginner's mind is one of the funnest and easiest things to share. Just last week I took a beginner down a local class II run. He was so excited he could hardly contain himself, but he also kept apologizing and saying, "You must be bored." He was torn between his own fun exploring the river, and worrying that it was too easy for me. I laughed and assured him it was actually one of my favorite little stretches, and just being on the water was interesting and fun. Right on cue, we saw a great blue heron up close, all legs and neck and chiseled beak, ambling through the shallow water and peering at us. The salmon flies were hatching, now and again fluttering like gigantic prehistoric insects around our boats. A set of baby ducklings hid behind the reeds in an eddy with their mother, peeping softly and huddling close to her.

I worked with my friend on catching eddies, reading water, and the rudiments of surfing. It's fascinating to watch somebody learn about the current, to see the glimmerings of comprehension and then the first lights come on with a massive grin. Throughout, I was busy looking at every eddy and wave as a place of learning, for him and for me. I suppose instead of doing all that I could have been thinking, "I've done hundreds of class V rivers all over the world and here I am wasting my time on a stupid class II run." But it was a beautiful river and I enjoy teaching. Best of all, I had a partner who was simply radiating enthusiasm and serving as the perfect reminder of the importance of beginner's mind. Should I have been learning less than him? How could I be bored with such a rich set of things to see and think about?

A concept shows its depth when its opposite is also insightful. From this point of view, consider what happens when you don't use beginner's mind.

20 years ago I met a guy who was a great slalom paddler, a national team member for years, and who had competed in several world championships. He'd moved out West and started coming to our whitewater rodeos. We welcomed him and everybody thought it was great to have a super paddler from a completely different background. I grilled him on slalom technique, asked zillions of questions and learned as much as I could.

To me, the amazing thing was the openness didn't go the other way, for instance, he wouldn't enter the free-style contests. In fact, he wouldn't even try any of the moves, even just for fun with a couple of us helping him. It wasn't an issue of ego; it was an issue of beginner's mind. He finally told me that he wouldn't do it because he couldn't stand not being in control when he paddled. "I hate feeling like a spazz," he added. All his control was based on the mindset and techniques of world class competition slalom. Mentally he wasn't flexible enough to let go, accept the temporary "spazz" and enjoy the process of learning something different.

The sad outcome was he couldn't learn what we were doing. He also told me he couldn't get himself even to try the moves because he couldn't stand not being really good at something. So he ended up doing the same things he'd always practiced. He was extremely skilled at them, but his rigidity prevented him from learning anything new. I've always felt bad about this, because none of my encouragement convinced him to join us. It was a shame – a great athlete who had lost the willingness to embrace the new. I'm not sure, but perhaps that lack of control was frightening to him. Perhaps he didn't want to face the simple fear that every beginner has and that he himself worked through in years past to get to his level of expertise. If the fear or dislike of beginning stops you, then the beginner's joy also is out of reach.

Sometimes you see both sides of beginner's mind in people's reactions. In my last column, I talked about some of the challenges I found on the North Fork of the Payette and its 15 miles of outstanding Class V whitewater. Among other things, these included handpaddling as well as doing long series of continuous runs at higher flows, leading to massive amounts of vertical drop and what I called my "Mozart experience" – feeling the entire length of the river, all its lines and waves and rapids, present in a single instant when I closed my eyes. All of these attempts came because I took to heart the idea of beginner's mind. I wanted to find new ways to look at something I was intimately familiar with. But, like my slalom acquaintance above, not everybody is drawn to that. Interestingly, several friends greatly disliked what I was doing, especially the hand-paddling, and aimed some heavy criticisms in my direction. I was even told by one friend that he wouldn't get on the river with me if I didn't have a paddle in my hands. He had his reasons, the primary one being that these were "meaningless stunts". He wouldn't listen to my reasons, which were the ones I described in the column, and those I've been talking about here. It's a free country, so he can believe what he wants. I think he finally and rather grudgingly accepted it when he watched me hand-paddle and nail the crux moves in Jacob's ladder, perfectly in control. It might still be a stunt, but it sure wasn't just flailing down the river. In my opinion he allowed himself to get stuck on a certain vision of kayaking, rather than thinking back to the passion of possibilities he felt when he began.

Beginner's mind is the lure of something different, and it unfolds when fascination and curiosity replace the fear of the unknown. These ideas don't just apply to difficult rivers. It's the same feeling that leads you to paddle new rivers, or try a new boat. It overlaps that unbearable itch to head out to the local run after work or school, and the times when you can't think of anything but having a paddle in your hand, or doing a cutback on a wave. It lives in the wild, tossing images that play through your mind for hours after you get home.

Beginner's mind simply suggests these feelings can be a part of everything we do. We shouldn't reserve them only for the places that are dramatically different, challenging, or unknown. And they are not just for the great playspots at their best levels. Each of these things evokes it, but the real understanding comes when you knock around with a five-year old along the river's edge. Then, you see just how wild and fascinating the simplest place can be, and you realize that all the things you've long since lost interest in are actually incredible, amazing wonders of the world. You don't have to be looking at a challenging run or some great freestyle move. It's your eyes and attitude that make each thing exactly what it is, or make it a doorway to greater possibilities.

Ironically, often beginners are in such a hurry to get better that they become impatient and even annoyed that they can't do something. When that happens, the beginner himself loses the best part of beginner's mind. Likewise, as we get increasingly skilled, that best part can easily be shoved aside by other concerns, such the anxiousness of a competition, the desire for sponsorship, the hint of ego, or simply getting in a rut. For those of us who keep learning, it is probably most important to remind ourselves that the better we are at something, the more we can gain from thinking back to the beginning.

I believe the key is never to allow learning to get old, and I think that kayakers are able to do that more than any other group because our love affair with water makes it harder for us to take things for granted. Or, to put it in another way, the passion is always there because the water is always changing, challenging, and delighting us.

All of these things are part of the concept of beginner's mind, and understanding them is a good way to ensure yourself of a lifetime of deep fun on rivers. So be careful not to get stuck up about what you know, or allow yourself to settle into a rigid view of things. Like the water, always flow from the old into the new. If you keep this up, you will learn more as a kayaker, your skills will expand, your fun will increase, and your appreciation of rivers will grow for an entire lifetime. Because after all, the river never stops, and if we continue on its path, neither will we.

***

A Different View of the River – Slalom Skills

I believe we can learn a great deal from rivers, whether it is physical skills, mental focus, or emotional perspective. Consider one place you can find a quiver of new skills even in class II whitewater: slalom paddling.

While I'm not a great advocate of racing, if you've never paddled on a slalom course, I highly recommend it. You don't have to race, all you have to do is get out and try to make the gates. I guarantee you will find even a simple course will teach you more in an afternoon than you are likely to learn in several years of running rivers. The course will immediately confront you with combinations of balance, strokes, and positions that you never would have dreamed of. Ferry angles become critical and small mistakes are magnified, forcing you to be aware of the current's complexity. Each move is a little puzzle that can be worked out, and each solution increases your sensitivity to the river's features, its power and cross currents, waves and eddy structure. By the end of the day a world will have opened up, and you will understand for the first time just how many lines there really are in a rapid. This realization presents you with a choice in every rapid thereafter – a you can float down the main tongue, or you can search for the river's secrets. Seek and ye shall find, play and apply what you learn to other rivers. You won't regret it.

Slalom has immediate application to river running. In fact, a slalom course is essentially a complex class IV or V line with a road map. The gates say "be here" and then "go there". If the course setter is good, every part of the sequence will tax your ability to read water and control your boat.

Usually when running a river, rapids seldom require more than a couple of moves. However, a slalom course will have 20 or 25 moves, one right after the other, so it demands a very high level of endurance and precision. It also requires you find a flowing line that connects the sequence of moves. A good racer will scout the course, then rip it. In a serious race, competitors can look all they want but they only get one practice run, which puts a premium on being able to convert what you see from the bank into what you must do on the river. Essentially, figuring out a slalom course uses the same skills as scouting and running a hard rapid.

Most of all, a slalom course typically has no consequences. If you miss a gate you might be annoyed, but it won't ruin your day. It's like sport climbing in this respect – you can push yourself and find the absolute limits of your control because the danger of injury has essentially been eliminated. That's a huge help in improving your skills – you have the green light to go for it. Take away the gates and add the consequences, and you have Class IV+ or V.

As good as slalom is for teaching, any tool also has its drawbacks. In the case of slalom it is the hyperfocus on control in the service of an aggressive racing mentality. In contrast, running rivers requires a certain flexibility of perception that can sit uneasily with the mindset slalom tends to create. Let me give you an example.

I met Rob Novotny when he was only 17 and a member of the Canadian junior national team. We hit it off from the start, and I found it interesting that although he was a very good paddler, nearly all his experience with rivers had been gate training and slalom racing on easy rivers. So, I invited him down to the Lochsa to introduce him to some of the best bigwater class IV in the world. The Lochsa is one of my nominations for the Whitewater Hall of Fame, which should include only rivers and no people at all. It's huge bouncy fun with great surf waves and big holes, very powerful, but relatively benign. And it's beautiful. Even at high water the river runs clean. You can see the rocks on the bottom as if looking through transparent liquid glass, and the water is so cold it burns your hands and face. It is whitewater heaven, in the clearest, cleanest water imaginable. Novotny was blown away.

We started by running Fish Creek, a small tributary of

the Lochsa that I would describe as the perfect introduction to class IV creek paddling. It's 100 feet per mile with big boulders, sharp eddies, tight drops and ledges, the kayaking version of a game of full-contact speed chess in the most beautiful place in the world: bishop – knight – queen – *checkmate*!

Novotny ripped the moves, boofed ledges, whipped into eddies, ferried above drops, and nailed the run. However, at first he kept nervously turning back and asking me, "What's around the corner? Where should I go?" I didn't answer his questions, but yelled, "catch an eddy and see for yourself!" That annoyed him, but quickly he was having too much fun to be annoyed. I wasn't being obnoxious; I just didn't want to steal the best of the experience from him. He had outstanding technical skills, but not the mindset of a whitewater paddler. My goal was for him to discover how the skills he already had could set him free. I knew we were on the right course when we reached the bottom and he said with a huge smile on his face, "Now I understand where slalom fits on the river."

Novotny was an extremely good kayaker, he won a spot on the Canadian national team and spent two seasons paddling on the World Cup circuit. He also had an openness for new experiences that chaffed at the bit. Slalom was fun, but once he confronted the bigger world of rivers, he wanted me to show him a few more. So later in the summer, I invited him down to the North Fork of the Payette, a river renown for its outstanding continuous, class V rapids. It was late July, the water was warm and at a medium-low level of about 2000 cfs. I had prepped him, saying we would scout carefully, take it rapid by rapid, and I'd help him with the lines. I assured him he had the ability to run the river, but that it would push him hard. If he wanted, he could portage any rapid that he didn't like. He was excited and apprehensive, but ready to give it a go.

Rob Lesser, one of the great paddlers in the history of the sport, met us at the put in. He knew Novotny strictly as a slalom paddler and was surprised to see him, "Novotny! What are you doing here?" "Well, Doug convinced me to give the

North Fork a try." "That's great!" said Lesser, who added cheerfully, "I'm sure you have the skills to survive."

Now Lesser meant that as a matter-of-fact compliment, but Novotny fixated on the word "survive". His face went blank for a few moments, then he scurried over to me and whispered, "Doug, he said I had the skills to … *survive*. What the hell have you gotten me into?" I told him don't worry, just get ready for an interesting day.

Novotny was as tense as anyone I've ever seen. It was a sight to behold. I thought he was going to blow a gasket and expected to see smoke coming out of the holes in his helmet. We'd done a pre-scout, but you just can't take the measure of the North Fork that way. The river goes and goes. Even the shortest rapids are hundreds of yards long, many of them continuous for a half mile, and there aren't any give-aways. Novotny handled everything great, but was in complete sensory overload the entire time. He portaged the upper part of Nutcracker, one of the largest rapids, got back in below and continued. I kept asking him if he wanted to stop and he'd say no. So I'd tell him the line in the next rapid and he'd nod, or else we'd get out and scout part of it. Then off we'd go into the wild flowing yonder.

Think about what he was doing. It's really a testament to his ability to adapt and his motivation, and especially to the remarkable skills he'd learned from slalom. Big water paddling is about as opposite from slalom as it's possible to get, yet he went from his race training, mostly on class II water, to a 17-mile Class V romp full of huge holes, pourovers, and crashing waves – and not a slalom gate in sight to tell him where to go. Solid whitewater with no road map. Or rather, he had to create his own road map. His mind wanted him to cut and slash his way, pick precise lines, but there was just too much. The river pounded his precision slalom edges like a jackhammer, overwhelming his sense of what a line was and what paddling meant. I wanted to show him the real stuff. The North Folk took care of that.

Finally, we stopped at Jacob's Ladder and Novotny decided to get out. He'd reached his limit. "I've had it. This was the hardest day of my life. I really appreciate the run, it's outrageous and amazing, but I've got to get out." He drove the shuttle vehicle down and watched through the rest of the run, then we had dinner and headed home. He chattered nonstop about the North Fork the entire six-hour drive back to Missoula. It changed his whole definition of kayaking. Slalom had trained his skills, but the Lochsa and North Fork Payette had shown him how they could be used.

Novotny called me sometime later and confided that he had had a headache for six solid days afterward. Then he asked, "When can we go again?"

Kayaking is full of new skills to learn. I recommend you practice a little slalom along the way, keeping in mind its best application is on rivers that run free, improvising your way and working with the flow. Rivers present us with nearly infinite variety, and slalom techniques immensely develop your ability to see and take advantage of the current's subtleties. But never confuse the techniques with the slalom mindset. Slalom is racing, and very few of us want to race down a river. Instead, we want to savor it, and the skills allow that. It's all in the application and your mindset. So take some time with the gates, then return to the river and be amazed yet again at how fun and complex it is; how much it can teach and how much you can learn. You won't regret it.

***

The Bond of the River

People normally don't talk about their kayaking in terms of ethics. However, in my experience kayaking is deeply ethical. One of the most powerful examples of this might be called the bond of the river.

Ethics and kayaking seem an odd couple because kayaking is a recreation. Typically, people are in it to have fun, do their own thing, and escape from the normal workaday world. Almost by definition ethics are serious business. For most rebellious kayaker types, it evokes the things that they try to get away from when they are recreating – like virtues, judgment, responsibilities, and obligations. This odd couple may even seem like two opposites – self-focused fun versus altruism.

Ethics enters because even when we kayak easy rivers there is an element of seriousness. Although the water is nearly always forgiving, there are possible dangerous consequences that can't be ignored. The danger and seriousness, and the commitment necessary to deal with them, transform the recreation into something greater.

You'll see this immediately if you answer the question of who you'd like to have as partners. What qualities do you think of? A few off the top of my head would be funny, thoughtful, honest, competent, concerned about others, loyal, committed, and willing to endure hardship. We could make a long list and it would vary from person to person, but in general those are the kinds of things that would be on it. Nearly every one of them is an aspect of ethical behavior. Some might be called virtues, but all of them also have to do with how the person treats others. In a word, we're describing the ethics of our ideal partner.

If we would like those things from our partner, then we had better be ready to give them ourselves. That actually is one of the fundamentals of ethics. You could be fancy and call it "reciprocity", or just note that it's the old golden rule. The fact is, if you want a good partner, then you'd better be one yourself.

The simplest ethical acts are things you learned as a kid, for instance taking turns. It doesn't matter whether it's a turn on the swing or surfing a wave. These are respect and care for others. They include going after a swimmer, helping with shuttles, getting lost gear back to its owner, or making room for somebody in an eddy. The most important one that underpins the others is helping those in need. This feeling, more than any other, forms the bond of the river.

I always took for granted that such things were bedrock attitudes in kayaking. Nobody ever told me. It seemed obvious they were needed out there, particularly when things got tough. It was also the attitude I saw in the older paddlers I started with, and it fit my view of the world. However, over the past few years I've seen some disturbing situations that suggest there are a lot of paddlers who don't think that way. Consider two examples.

At the popular artificial playspot in Missoula, Brennan's wave, last year a novice swam and none of the ten or twelve excellent paddlers in the eddy went after him. This wasn't a benign swim – the water was high and fast, there are trees in the current directly below, and the bank downstream is rip-rapped and covered with dense brush with the current running through it. There are only a few places where it's possible to get out without struggling through thick willows in swift water. It would certainly be possible to get killed there, or at least have a really bad time. The one person who went after the swimmer was just putting on the river in a C-1. He chased him down, gathered his gear, and helped him out. I arrived just after it happened and came upon the C-1 paddler, who shook his head at the selfishness and lack of camaraderie he had witnessed. Nodding toward the eddy, he said "I just hope I never have to rely on any of those guys."

The second example is even more troublesome. A few years ago a friend of mine was surfing a big wave on a different river with a group that included professional paddlers from sponsored teams. Several paddlers were out on the wave together when one of them did a fast cutback, shot over and speared my friend hard with the bow of his boat. My friend flipped and was immediately swept downstream, struggling to roll, and in such severe pain he nearly blacked out. He struggled for several minutes until he made it upright and got to the bank a good half mile down from the wave. As many as eight kayakers witnessed the incident. Nobody helped. The guy who speared him just pulled back into the eddy and kept surfing as if nothing had happened.

It took my friend a long time to pull his boat back upstream, and then he lay in his truck in a lot of pain for several hours; meanwhile, the dudes kept surfing and nobody paid any attention to the missing paddler. He drove to the emergency room after he noticed he was peeing blood. The doctors found he had cracked ribs, a partially ruptured spleen, and internal bleeding. He was freaking out when he called me for advice, because he had no medical insurance and the doctors were talking about having to remove his spleen. I tried to calm and reassure him. Over the next few weeks they backed off the surgery while he racked up large medical bills from the exams.

So what about the dude who speared him? Although confronted, the dude never apologized until a pointed discussion with his sponsor laid down the law: he could apologize and help pay the medical expenses, or he would be cut from sponsorship. That would probably have been the end of him as a professional kayaker, because what other company would ever want to be associated with that behavior? So with that ultimatum, he complied. However, he never did apologize to my friend's face. It took an additional ultimatum over the next several months for him to fax what can only be described as a pseudo-apology. My friend showed it to me. The main line was "I'm sorry you got hurt" – as if some outside force had done it without the dude's knowledge or participation, like Zeus throwing a lightning bolt from Mt. Olympus or a comet hitting the earth. It took the threat of losing his sponsorship and the damning effect that would have on his résumé even to say that. Just so we're clear about it, most people would have said, "I'm sorry I speared you and sorry I didn't help after afterwards. It was bad judgment. I hope you forgive me." Actually, a normal ethical person would have taken off after the other guy, regardless of whose fault it was.

Only a little of the money ever made it. The dude had the funds to travel, party, and paddle all around the country, but couldn't cough up anything to pay for the injuries he had inflicted. And frankly, it's not really an issue of him being a professional. The exact same point would apply for any able-bodied paddler. It's just that one might expect a professional to take the bond even more seriously, rather than ignoring it in such a casual way in a situation where serious harm and injury were caused. Further, he wasn't alone and he surely could point to the others who were there, professional and nonprofessional, who acted the same way.

So what about ethics? I'm not picking on sponsored paddlers in general, because the overwhelming majority of them are solid guys, and any group has its outliers. I'm just pointing out that in this situation where all the paddlers should have been looking out for each other, there was nothing but selfishness. There was no loyalty, no commitment, and no help for others. It was the negation of the bond of the river – and all for a few minutes of surfing.

It's one thing to have an attitude like that on a less difficult river, but it's quite another on a hard river. As the consequences become more serious the ethical principles become sharper. At the upper end of the sport where one is dealing with hard Class V and VI in uncompromising surroundings, it is possible to reach a kind of absolute purity of ethics. Typically, the attitudes reflect that. The partners are closer friends, and have a deep, even fierce sense of loyalty to each other.

I can say without hesitation that I have and always will put my life on the line to help partners – and I've found that true of nearly every serious paddler. It was seen last summer when Conrad Fourney's partners jumped into a class V rapid to try and pry him off the obstruction he was pinned on underwater. Conrad died, but his partners gave him everything they had short of their own lives, and that's the way it has to be. The same is true of Dugal Bremner some years ago, trapped in a siphon, which two of his partners actually got sucked through underwater while trying to free him. Or Pablo Perez, who was wedged under an unseen log in the middle of a drop, with two partners repeatedly jumping into the middle of a serious and dangerous place, attempting to grab and pull him loose. Or Tim Gavin, where even after he had died the rescue team risked their lives to recover his body. That is the bond of the river. It binds us together even in death.

In my own career, while I loved the fun of freestyle and the challenge of whitewater, these other aspects are what most drew me to harder runs, and especially expeditions. There, I found the purity of friendship and commitment. I found a precious diamond. There was courage, honesty, and self-sacrifice for partners, while working toward a shared goal. I looked right in their eyes and knew exactly what they were thinking. There was no doubt, no hesitation, and no bullshit. I have never been to war and never been a soldier, but friends of mine did multiple tours in the Special Forces, or were Marines and Rangers. They each told me they appreciated kayaking because of intensity of whitewater, and the sense of loyalty and camaraderie that their teams gave them. I understand that.

Kayaking is a sport. It is recreation and fun, but it can be much more. Class V is essentially synonymous with the likelihood of injury or death if a substantial mistake is made, and an arena like that can pull us to the greatest heights of moral behavior and the very best things we are capable of.

It may be that the ethics are clearest in serious whitewater, but it is in the easiest whitewater, and particularly with beginners, that our ethics may have even greater consequences. What we show those beginners defines what the sport is and what it will become in the future. It shouldn't require a desperate life and death situation to understand the importance of treating other people with the care and respect each of them deserve. I would hope it is self-evident that when we understand the bond of the river, we will also understand the place of ethics in kayaking.

***

An Ode to a Special River

Learning the moods of a river is one of the great pleasures of kayaking. The first few years, you're all excited about the whitewater, or the surfing and playspots. After several season watching local rivers ebb and flow, a different feeling arises because you've started to learn the cycle of the river, seeing it as the living force of the surrounding landscape.

Here in western Montana and Idaho the river's cycle is a celebration of the seasons. The waters lie low under the frozen ice and gradually wake as winter's grip turns to spring. The melting snow up in the high mountains swells the flow, set loose in earnest by the first hot days and warm rains in May. Spring runoff is a frenzy of racing water that ebbs toward summer, until the skeleton of the riverbed shows itself, revealing the boulders that formed the rapids. Heading into fall and early winter, the last water begins to freeze, and the cycle is ready to repeat.

Of all the rivers I've ever run, one of the greatest is the North Fork of the Payette, about 60 miles north of Boise, Idaho. A full run has the title "top to bottom" – 15 miles and 1700 feet of romping class IV+ and V+ at regular flows. The North Fork's cycle is not quite normal, because it is dammed. But amazingly, releases are managed in a way that amplifies some of the best qualities of the cycle of seasons. One of these is making the river's summer moods linger from late June all the way to October.

The North Fork Payette can never really be summed up. You can experience it from outer limits big water cascading along at 30+ miles per hour, to measured steep creeking down what seems like an infinitely long boulder garden. There are so many rapids and they vary so much across water levels, that it's almost impossible to memorize details. That keeps it fresh no matter how many times you run it.

Over the years, I've run the river in every way I could think of, for the challenge and fun, the difficulty, and for the intimacy with the water. Three of the most challenging experiences were high water descents, handpaddling, and doing multiple top to bottoms in a day.

At high water above 5000 cfs, the North Fork defies description. It has a narrow, steep riverbed, so when it fills up there isn't any place for all that water to go except downstream as fast as it can. The huge boulders try to slow it, but all they succeed in doing is riling it up into a tumble of exploding waves and mounding holes. Even from the bank it's breathtaking. But when you put on, you shift into a parallel universe. The water becomes a beast of a different order, like a hungry T-Rex stomping downhill trying to catch its dinner. Reflexes honed for lower levels don't work, and you play catch-up as the water accelerates away from you. We ran the river repeatedly at high flows, always coming to the bottom with our eyes wide open and shaking our heads. The height of my own experience was running a number of complete top to bottoms at nearly 7000cfs, including Jacob's ladder and Golf Course, which together have to be one of the single most beautiful and powerful rapids anywhere in the world.

Talking about the highs also means mentioning the lows. My low was getting massacred on another such run in 1995, plastered at high speed on the front of a boulder. That hit, together with the frantic scramble for my life afterwards through another 300 yards of class V+ while paralyzed on one half of my body, left some indelible memories of what water can do. But that's part of learning the river.

Handpaddling was another step in the natural progresssion of exploring the river. Frankly, handpaddling looks stupid from the bank, but I don't care how it looks, because it gives an intimacy with the water that can't be found any other way. You have almost no power compared to the current, so you have to make up for that with your sensitivity. Angle and anticipation are everything. Your hands are directly in contact with the water and you feel the current threads, the bubbles, the quick shudders from the rocks whipping by underneath. You caress the wild beast, enmeshed with its power. The river opened up in a subtler way and I realized handpaddling gave me two versions of an all time great river. It was possible to run everything cleanly at any of the normal levels, and even do top to bottoms at almost the highest flows. But at the upper levels, I reached a point where I was merely going where the river put me instead of being able to choose the line. I decided I'm not out there just to survive, but to be the river's respectful partner in flow.

Another step was multiple runs. Bob McDougall did the first ever vertical mile in 1988, three top to bottoms, which I thought was outrageous. I followed that with 6000 feet in a day by running the center five-mile section seven times. Think about it, 5280 feet of whitewater. That's a lot of drop. Splay it out into rapids, waves and holes, lead-ins and run-outs. Doing things like that force you to look at barriers differently and not to accept what you thought were limits.

A couple of years later I tried doing two vertical miles of whitewater in a day, six top to bottoms. That's 90 miles of class V, 10,600 feet of drop. It's a distance that requires you use different measures, like ten Empire State Buildings, three El Capitans, the distance from basecamp to the summit of Mt. Everest. It was for the challenge and the sheer mind-bending perspective, for the training, and for the aesthetics of knowing the river as a unitary run. There's a whole universe out there that doesn't care about our human limits, and I wanted to give it a look.

Several younger friends came along because the idea excited them too. We started at 5:30am, with a thick fog over the river. Big holes would rush out of the mist, and if you didn't know where you were, it was a scramble. At 7:30 after we finished the first run, my younger friends had second thoughts and did every other one. At 9pm after five complete runs, I knew that if I went ahead on the sixth it would get dark about halfway down. I had a vision of being enticed to finish number six in total darkness, which suddenly struck me as a good reason to quit. My hands were blistered up and raw, I was exhausted and alone, so I called it a day after 8500 vertical feet.

Multiple runs are not just a grunt, yo-yoing up and down the river. It is inspiring flowing with all that power around you, like taking part in the most intricate, lovely music or the most beautiful dance with nature. The greatest pleasure is closing your eyes, feeling dozens of long rapids and thousands of moves flowing through you like the water itself. The composer Mozart said that he had entire symphonies come to him in a single instant, hearing all the different instruments, harmonies, and melodies all at once in his mind. I can close my eyes and feel the entire 15 miles of the North Fork in my body, the lines, paddle strokes and boat angles, the wild flowing water all the way down like a symphony. I found my Mozart experience on the river. How can I not love the North Fork for giving me that priceless opportunity?

The river is always changing, and it always has more to offer. I've only scratched the surface. The highest I ran it was almost 7000 cfs, but the North Fork went up to over 8000 in the 1940s, and will probably get up there again sometime. One January day in the 1990s, it looked like that would happen. There was a freak warm rain on top of a sizeable snow pack, and for a few days the rivers went crazy. I tried to make it down but all the highways were washed out. It turned out it was a false alarm for the North Fork, as the flood levels were on the South Fork Payette, while the North Fork just got high, but not to flood stage. So we'll just have to wait a while longer. And I'm sure it's possible to do two vertical miles in a day. Six top to bottoms in a day. I think that's a good challenge for some young hot-shot stud.* All those Empire State Buildings worth of whitewater, and the Mozart experience of your life. I did a vertical mile of hand-paddling and high water runs, but my Boise friend Jim Grossman took the high water handpaddling farther than I did, claiming that playing the holes was a constant rodeo all the way down, until he got stuck under a log near the bottom of Golf Course – but that's another story.

Every river that you will ever run has a distinct personality at each level. It moves through its own beautiful cycle, and it will always teach you something new if your mind is open. The music and dance are there, the intimacy and laughter with your friends. There never will be an end to that if you retain your beginner's mind.

Now go and have some fun.

***

* A few months after this essay was published in 2006, three young hotshots did six top to bottoms in a day: Fred Coriell, Ryan Casey, and Bryan Fletcher. My hat is off to them. Bryan told me that he had tendinitis for a month afterwards.

Paddler, Know Thyself

Last month I wrote about the pleasure of understanding how rivers change through the seasons, and how it leads to a huge change in your awareness. After only a year or two of paddling, you start closely watching the snow pack, the rainfall and temperatures, and gradually become aware of a river's moods. At first this knowledge is purely in terms of your favorite spots – you know you can surf a particular wave when the water gets to a certain level, or a certain rapid fills in and some great move develops. Over time, it expands into hundreds of such details, and they branch out into the tributaries and sister rivers of a watershed. Knowing each river's quirks and gestures makes them feel like old friends. Pulled along by your passion, your kayaking becomes a way to understand the river's personality and how it focuses the forces of the surrounding land.

There's another way this awareness and understanding can be directed. Turned around, the personalities of your favorite rivers can be used as a mirror. A great Greek philosopher once counseled, "know thyself". Rivers provide an infinite number of ways to do that.

What you seek in kayaking reflects who you are. You may love freestyle moves or surfing, steep creeking or cruising. Class III may be your limit and you aren't interested in anything harder. Or, you may want to cut your teeth on the hardest things around and still reach for more. For at least 15 years, each season a group of my old friends loved taking a four or five day wilderness trip together down the Middle Fork of the Salmon every year, laughing, ribbing each other, running rapids and sitting around a campfire as the stars shone overhead.

When I ask people what they get from kayaking, they mention things like the traveling, friendship, and beautiful places. Some people mention the thrills and exhilaration. The young men usually say it's a blast, awesome, and challenging. The young women often stress that they've found confidence, overcome fear, and become physically strong.

All those are important, but I'm going to propose a few other things to think about. In doing this, I'm only mentioning the things that I've found valuable. My kayaking has run the gamut of playing, first descents, competition, expeditions, and solos. Throughout most of my career, it also has been nestled within my roles as a professional scientific editor, a father of five, husband, and running a business with a lot of employees. Because I've had to balance those different worlds over the years, I'm a strong believer that each of us should regularly examine our lives as time goes on. I believe that knowing ourselves, our weaknesses and strengths, is the first step toward some kind of wisdom. It's an ongoing search for ideals.

It's both a simple fact and a profound truth that the fun of kayaking comes in part from the potential danger of the river. Another way to say that is, the reason it is so much fun is because you're dealing with real consequences. If there were no consequences to our actions and you didn't have to worry about getting thrashed or worse, then it wouldn't mean as much to you. Things can get ugly in Class III; you don't need to be in class V to have a really bad experience. So the first question I ask about knowing yourself is, where does the danger fit into your life?

The nature of moving water and rivers underscores every decision you make. A river is the physical flow of time, and nowhere else can you see so clearly how one decision sweeps into another. An early lesson the river teaches is that you have to be engaged at every moment because even a small lapse can snowball quickly into a huge problem. That's where the excitement comes from – the interplay between your skills and the river's complexity and power. When the ante is raised, this is also where the anxiety and even fear may come from. This is why you get satisfaction from making a hard move or making the line, just right, in a big rapid - or any rapid that is challenging to you. Of course, danger has other much nastier sides and the key is finding the balance.

For those people who paddle difficult whitewater, a second related question I ask about knowing yourself is, what are the things you get from the sport that balance the danger? Let me point-blank it: is your fun enough to die for? I think not, but some people act as if it is. Realistically, the more time we spend on something and especially the more potential danger it carries, the better our reasons should be for doing it.

As fantastic and as exciting as paddling is, since those extra consequences are right there, you need to consider your river choices not only as a paddler, but as a person. As a father or son, as a mother, daughter or friend. Part of my own answer to the philosopher's counsel, is to look for the things that push my understanding. Not just physical skills and knowledge about rivers, but the effects on my judgment and things that I can share with the people I love. When I talk with younger people in the sport about what experiences they valued the most, they mention character-building, like overnight trips where things didn't go right and they wound up spending the night sitting on a rock in the jungle. They mention traveling together, tempers coming out, and learning to live with other people. All of these are good answers and are strong steps in the direction of self knowledge. But again, these days, some talented kids progress so quickly that they run hard Class V and huck 80 foot waterfalls as teenagers, which are potentially life threatening actions. The bigger the consequences, the better the reasons should be. A cliché like "he died doing what he loved" is a weak answer for parents who spent 20 years nurturing their son's growth, or for his friends who are left with a hole in their own lives. For young talented people who are getting sponsorship and "living the dream", it probably is much harder even to see any value in the questions I propose. It's much easier to be wrapped up in youthful enthusiasm and the outer rewards they get through their skills. Yet, the questions remain, and once the cheering and sponsorship stop, those questions will force themselves into the forefront – where they probably should have been all along.

One good answer many people have, without really thinking about it as an answer, is that they take the enthusiasm they have for the river and apply it to the other things they do.

The river charges them up, eases their frustrations, and makes them into better people. That infectious good will and passion are worth their weight in gold. Who would you rather be with, somebody who's uninspired about life, or a person brimming with good spirits?

Another answer that is harder to apply because it requires deliberate attention, is mindfulness. You can't paddle something even halfway difficult and not be forced to pay close attention to the subtleties of the features and current. A single experience of being completely focused on the moment will remain with you, vividly and convincingly, for your whole life. If you add a little objective danger with real consequences to this, it becomes a compelling, potent brew. The simple reaction is to want more of it, to hunger for it with the same intensity you have in a passionate love affair. However, it is important to take this a step further. That is, to see your mindfulness on the river as an inspiration for what you can do when fully engaged. It is an awakening; it gives you a glimpse of the kind of person you could be. So as an ideal, take the same care that you have in running rapids at your limit, and apply it to everything you can off the river.

Think about a few of the consequences in normal life. The consequences usually aren't as direct as getting hammered in a rapid, but that doesn't make them any less important. Consider, for instance, being mindful about fairness and having respect for others. If you impulsively insult somebody, flip them the bird in traffic, cavalierly treat a person like he or she doesn't exist, think of those things in terms of a kayaking decision in hard class V. They all have consequences, even though you might not see them because they are inside the other person. They are there, and just as surely, they remain inside you as well, reflecting who you are. Ask yourself this question from time to time about the mindfulness you love so much when paddling: is our goal really to be mindful on the river and mindless off it?

A final issue is perspective. As intense and meaningful as paddling may be at times, no matter how important kayaking is to you, and no matter how far you push your skills, the hardest things you'll ever do won't be on the river. I've pushed myself very, very hard in kayaking. I've done a lot of first descents in the US and overseas expeditions, soloed a number of top end runs, done 8500 vertical feet of class V in a day, run rapids that nobody else would touch, gotten badly injured several times, and utterly thrashed on exploratory trips that turned out to be fiascos.

But the hardest things I've ever done weren't on the water. They were being a parent, having a job and raising five children, being a good husband, and taking care of my father when he was dying. They were dealing with the suicides of my best friend and of my younger brother, who left his own five young children with a hole in their lives that I could never fill. Those are the hardest things I've ever done.

I love kayaking because it's the funnest, most challenging, wildest sport I've ever found. However, looking back on the last 25 years I value it most for how it fits into my life and what it means. Paddling can be a great sport and recreation, but it can also deepen the best qualities you have as a person. Know thyself, a great philosopher once said. The rivers we love are that philosopher's equal - and more - if we only listen.

***

Adventure, Niagara Falls, and "Crazy"

I think it's likely all kayakers have been told at some point that they are crazy. It doesn't matter if you paddle on lakes and easy rivers, or over waterfalls and difficult whitewater. Somebody along the way will say you stepped over the bounds of good sense, and are nuts or have a death wish.

What people consider insane is a question of their comfort zone and whether they are willing to step out of it. To do an adventure sport, you have to enjoy stepping up to the limits of your experience and looking over the edge, hopefully carefully enough that you don't go too far before you realize it. Everybody has different appetites for newness and weighs consequences differently, so there's no magic edge that everybody agrees on. In the end, you can convince yourself that something is actually quite doable and even fun while it sounds perfectly insane to others. It's worth remembering too, that no matter how well you think you have a new stunt figured out, things don't necessarily turn out the way you expect.

In any case, the next time somebody calls you the "C" word and shakes his head, have some ammunition ready. Here are some counterexamples of certifiable nut cases to trot out, and in comparison to them, even the wildest kayaker will look conservative. We're sane, I swear!

The history of Niagara Falls is about as colorful as any place in whitewater annals and many of the best stories come from it. You get your loonies and the occasional fruitcake who actually has a bead on the truth. All of them, for one reason or another, gravitate toward spectacular places like the falls.

The escarpment that makes the falls is a beautiful dark basalt layer about 160 feet tall. The river runs strong and wide there, plummeting over the edge in a massive cataract that has inspired people for hundreds of years.

If the falls are big, the dreams of some people are even bigger. There are the legendary stories, most of them true, of the guy or gal in a wooden barrel washing over the edge and disappearing into the frothing base of the plunge pool. Most have been killed, but a surprising number of them have actually made it - which is amazing if you consider the hazards of falling 160 feet - that's 16 stories - and having thousands of tons of water piling down on top of you, yet having faith that your body will survive the pummeling and the barrel that you are in will carry you to safety.

There have been broken wrists and legs, concussions and bruises, and a great many people have washed out dead. Others had their barrels smashed and their bodies were never found. When you stand there and look at that mighty waterfall, the question naturally arises: What on earth could they have been thinking? It sounds like the proverbial suicidal stunt. How could you really think that you could do this sort of thing and live?

Anybody who has ever jumped off a 50 or 60 foot bridge into the water knows that you hit really hard. You can get your shoes blown off, or your feet badly bruised, even when you hit right. If you hit wrong, you'll pay dearly for it. For the excitable or those with a screw or two loose, it's fun, but after a couple of times I guarantee you start thinking seriously about the sanity of the thing. Professional high divers sometimes dive from over a hundred feet and more. And once, a friend of mine from high school by the name of Shawn jumped off a cliff that turned out to be almost 200 feet high. It was an impulsive jump into a cool and invitingly deep pool, but he hadn't really intended on doing something so - well, crazy. His pal, whose name was Jet, tried to stop him, but Shawn had jumped off of every sort of bridge and cliff into rivers and lakes, he was a gymnast, rock climber and kayaker, and probably missed his calling as a stuntman for James Bond films. In any case, he had a good claim to knowing what he was doing. "I was clear as a bell before I jumped," he told me years later. "I knew I could make it."

He was off and flying before he questioned himself, rapidly shrinking to ant-like size as Jet watched in horror. He finally hit - perfectly - but surfaced face down doing the dead man's float. By the time Jet was able to climb down to the pool, Shawn had dragged himself out of the water and was staggering down the trail, white as a sheet and bleeding from both ears and his nose. However, Shawn then proved himself totally sane by asking three simple questions.

"Where am I?"

"You're in Hawaii," replied Jet.

"Do I have any money?" asked Shawn.

"Yes you have money," replied Jet.

And after a few seconds thinking these answers over, Shawn asked a critical question that separates the sane from the insane: "Why did I jump?"

"I don't know, but let's get to a hospital quick."

I'd like to point out that clearly Shawn was fully rational even in his badly concussed state. He wasn't mentally unbalanced, he just made an impulsive decision. Fortunately he was one tough guy.

The hospital scene that followed is also informative about the separation between your normal decision that turns out badly, and full-bore craziness. Jet sat in the emergency room for some time as the doctor looked over Shawn. Finally, the doctor emerged with a grave look on his face.

"Is he okay?" asked Jet.

"Yes," said the doctor, "but I'd like to ask you a question." He looked thoughtfully at Jet for a few moments, then leaned forward and asked in a low voice, "Does your friend have any ... psychiatric problems?"

Taken aback, Jet answered, "No, none at all."

"He hasn't indicated any wish to, uh…, kill himself?"

Shocked, Jet blurted out, "God no, we just didn't think the cliff was so high."

Well, it turned out that the falls Shawn had jumped off of was regularly used by suicidal people and quite a number had been blown by the wind directly into the cliff as they fell. It had been a calm day when Shawn jumped. He landed perfectly and survived. He is a happy and successful businessman to this very day. Chalk it up as a bad decision, teetering on the verge of folly or madness, but with the important difference that he survived it.

So let us get back to Niagara Falls and those who decided it was a perfectly sane thing to float over. You have to tip your hats to those who took the plunge and came out alive at the bottom. Impulsively jumping into a barrel and flying over the edge of the falls, a la Shawn's jump, is maybe an understandable decision for a strong, adventuresome young man or woman. But meticulously planning a feat that turns out to be one's final exit from this life is either very dumb, or nuts.

Maybe it's the natural bent most of us have toward the macabre - the spectacle of weirdness and certain horrific ends, but when you get right down to it the failures at Niagara are what are most impressive. A miraculous success may inspire our wonder, but a disastrous and spectacular failure is where the action is. So here are a few of those "almost-made-it" runs that separate us from the true eccentric nutsos. These guys are beyond the pale, smack dab in the middle of weirdness, and in a word - crazy.

The physics of falling 160 feet is pretty simple and you learn it in a first physics course. The basics are summed up in two simple equations. For the less mathematically minded, what these equations amount to is that the farther you fall, the faster you go until you reach terminal velocity. There, at about 120 miles per hour, the air resistance slowing you down exactly offsets the acceleration from gravity speeding you up.

When you fall 160 feet or so you don't quite make it to terminal velocity, but you are tootling along faster than gramma's old Ford does - about 70 mph at the bottom. When you're in a river, you also are falling with all that water at your back, and when a gallon of water falls that far it hits with something like the crack of a big masonry brick heaved off an 18 story building. The water may not be quite as hard, but in a river there's a lot of it. The Niagara River has 50,000 to 100,000 cubic feet a second pounding over the falls, and each cubic foot of water weighs in at about 40 pounds. That's three million pounds per second, or about 1500 tons coming down and hitting the bottom at 70 miles per hour. It's hard to fathom that power. Imagine 50,000 sacks of Eco-Compost raining down on your head every second, a bulldozer falling on top of you with every tick of the clock, or a cement parking garage collapsing every 20 seconds.

Our heroes are not daunted by such thoughts. In fact, they are convinced that they know exactly what to do about the hazards. So one sign of the touched is that they never dwell on the negative. It either never occurs to them, or maybe they deny it outright, but more likely, they think they have figured some way to finagle around the problems. Confidence is theirs; they are right and do not fear. And that is how they so blithely and confidently cross the divide to meet their undoing.

A number of people have gone off the falls in wooden barrels. Anne Taylor was the first, and was grappled out of the frothing waters below the falls by a boatman, having suffered a broken arm and ribs. Others followed, some successful and many not.

One guy, George Stahakis, thought he had it iced. He reckoned that the main problems were having the barrel get broken by the impact and then drowning, or else being pummeled under in the backwash and running out of air before you could surface. So, he planned and thought and finally con-structed a bombproof steel container weighing nearly a ton that would withstand the huge force of the falls. He heavily padded the inside - no broken barrel and no broken bones for him. To top it off, he solved the problem of being held under water by installing several tanks of compressed air in the capsule. A six hour air supply should be plenty, he thought.

The fateful day came. Full of confidence, he had him-self sealed in the capsule and was pushed into the river above the falls. Over he went as the onlookers shuttered and some cheered. His metal craft disappeared at the bottom and ... didn't come up. Well, no matter. After all, he had that six-hour air supply.

Twenty-four hours later his capsule appeared, bobbing in the swirling waters below the falls. They opened it and there he was. Not a broken bone. All his limbs were intact, he had easily survived the fall. As the clock ticked past six hours with him pinned to the bottom in his one-ton capsule, he had had plenty of time to contemplate the one critical error in his calculations.

Another guy had it all figured out too. Charles Stephens' solution to the padding was to rig up an elastic harness that fit under his arms and around his waist and feet. Suspended within his specially built barrel, he would be impervious to broken limbs. Mindful of the hazards of heavy steel capsules, he wanted a light but strong wooden barrel that would easily float. He also had another idea to avoid tumbling out of control. After falling 160 feet, it's much better to land upright on one's feet, as it were, and minimize the force. Hitting sideways could easily destroy the barrel and also beat you against the side, breaking your bones or killing you, as happened to so many intrepid Niagara barrelers. So, for these and perhaps other reasons he thought it was better to stay upright, and for that he needed ballast in the bottom of the barrel. There's lots of ways to have ballast, you can load the bottom with rocks or lead or you could do what he did, which was to strap an anvil to his feet.

He was sealed into his barrel and went over the edge, certain of his plan's success. The barrel fell straight and true, all 160 feet to the roiling water below. It quickly came out of the backwash and was found shortly afterwards. The bottom was blown out. When curious rescuers peered inside the remaining shell all they found were two arms, secured into the harness. Neither the anvil or the armless body were ever recovered.

And barrelers don't have a lock on the best attempts. In 1985, as reported by the Darwin Awards committee, a daredevil named Robert constructed a homemade rocket-parachute contraption and rode a jet ski over the falls at full throttle. He planned to ignite the rocket to shoot him away from the falls, then open the parachute. He envisioned himself landing softly in the river below, raising his hands in triumph before the astonished tourists as he was fished out by the Maid o' the Mist tour boat. It was an awesome plan and almost everything worked. He shot down the little rapids above the falls at breakneck speed, chattering along over the waves working hard to keep the jetski on course. Just imagine the noise and excitement as you roar along! You're totally committed and every nerve tingles, adrenaline shoots through your body. You've never felt more alert! You crank the throttle wide open and the power of the engine drives you toward the yawning chasm! The edge looms closer and closer - *this is it* - until you shoot off the falls and fly through space toward the horizon, gravity suddenly suspended below you as the jet ski falls behind. However, reaching back to ignite the rocket, Robert found it wet. It failed to ignite and his parachute didn't deploy. The tourists were very impressed. Bystanders said his body was recovered from the river below by the Maid o' the Mist's crew. Wow!

Craziness comes in degrees. For the sake of perspective though, it's helpful to compare the sane things we kayakers do to the crazy things people do who really are out of it. We can rest easy, assured that we're not like them. After all, we've got it all figured out, don't we?

***

The Real Shit: Why I Paddle Class V
(1996)

Back in 1996, a kayaker named Trip Kenny was studying why people kayaked hard whitewater. He was in graduate school in sociology and posed the following question in several kayaking chat rooms, seeking answers from fellow paddlers:

"Why do you guys paddle class five? Why do you fling yourself over huge drops, through monster holes, into places that by all rights should kill you deader'n dirt?? What if you mess up?? What really keeps you going over those horizon lines? (be honest, kids)."

My friend Jim Snyder saw the posting and sent it to me, asking for a good answer. I mulled it over for a while and finally sent him the following essay.

It is a personal answer to Trip's question. We all know by definition Class five is dangerous and risky, with the possibility of injury or even death, so it's a good question to ask, and I hope everybody who does such things has a good answer for him or herself.

For myself, I thought there was some confusion in the original question. People come to the river with different motives. The problem with answering the question as it is stated, is that people look back and give justifications in hindsight, instead of looking at all the steps they took to get to where they are. There's a progression in anybody's career, whether it is the guy who finds his fun and comfort surfing waves on the local play run, or the people who end up striving for the edge. That progression isn't something you can foresee when you start, and it isn't something you sum up in a few words at the end.

It also seems pretty obvious that for each of us the reasons we started the sport change as we continue. Our first excitement becomes focused on certain things. Fun may solidify into confidence, then aggression. That's usually the point when you step into hard class four and the beginnings of class five. Sooner or later this gets toned by caution as a near miss or two gets you thinking. An accident may change the aggression to doubt or fear. Some people quit pushing at that point, others work their way out of it and start pushing again. But the point is, we've changed because of these things. We're never the same afterwards.

If we're around the sport for a while, we become aware of consequences that look over our shoulders when we head into hard rapids. We keep going because we've learned how to use our experience and skill to deal with them. I know a lot of excellent paddlers, and none of them believe they are going to get hurt if they take their normal care. They will admit it might be *possible* in general, but they don't think it will happen on *this* run. If we paddle well, we know we have a large measure of control over what happens, and we also have faith that if something comes up, we have the skills to figure it out. We also accept that class five means serious consequences are possible, and that there is at least some uncertainty in what they are and when they might appear. That is really the definition of challenge and adventure. I think if they weren't, a lot of us would find something else to do. So the danger and the uncertainty are necessary parts. In a nutshell, it says, this is reality. Everyone learns something when the chips get laid down and the river calls your hand. Even the cockiest guy can learn something he won't doubt. Real consequences have a certain authority.

Over the years, our paths go in many directions and it seems to me a big part of the draw is that we don't actually know where they'll lead. That also helps heighten the sense of adventure, and that very uncertainty is part of what is so enticing about the game. Experience is a great teacher, probably the best, so no matter which path we take it leaves its mark on us. To my mind, one of the best things about rivers is they are the living essence of movement and change – and we can't help but change as we travel with them.

So overall, it seems to me the problem here is that Trip's question is really backward. None of us started out doing what he's talking about, so we've got to go back to the beginning for the answers to make sense. The meaning comes from what's happened along the way.

Ultimately, I think all answers are personal, so the following is a personal sketch of one path, at a particular time during my career. Everybody takes their own path, but hopefully others will see some of themselves here, as well as places where we differ. Since we all learn and change over time, our answers change. At least that's been true for me.

***

I started out paddling because I loved the water. I learned the basic skills and after a couple of times on the river, found it was the wildest, funnest, most playful, and beautiful damn sport I'd ever done. The people were great, the rivers were beautiful and every horizonline stirred all the fun and questions anew. It was challenging, exciting and there seemed no limit to what I could do or where I could go. By my second or third time on the river, I was hooked. By the end of my first year, I was a fanatic.

I ran my first class five after I'd been paddling about two months. I didn't know very much, but as they say, maybe ignoreance is bliss. I'd been told the rapid was unrunnable, and at first I believed that. But after looking closely at the current and features, I suddenly realized there was a straightforward line in an otherwise class six drop. The key was seeing past the intimidation around the line. I committed, and ended up running it twice with no difficulties. It was a little scary, sitting in the eddy above and feeling the river surge beneath me. But what led me to paddle over that horizonline was a quiet sense of certainty. I knew what I'd seen. The mindblower came afterwards: realizing if you looked just right you could find a thread that carried you through all the dangers, right into the heart of the river. I'll never forget that feeling. The river opened up and beckoned so enticingly, so exquisitely, that I just had to follow. I couldn't help it. Somehow, it had to do with seeing something true and deep about the water and myself.

So I had a new goal that added something even more compelling to the fun and excitement. By the end of the first year, I was doing class 5 with regularity, paddling with the best guys in the area. With good role models to learn from and great rivers to run, you can bootstrap yourself up pretty quickly. I went looking for new places, mostly steep creeks tucked away in remote canyons. Thing led to thing. Exploring, topo maps, recon, first attempts, failures, waterfalls, rappells, complex portaging - all to find wild lines down beautiful sparkling streams. I shared them with my best buddies, made new friends, committed to little adventures. Sometimes we'd get thrashed but we always came back. Who could ask for a better world to live in? I found a place clean and pure, where the sun and snowmelt laughed with you as you scouted, then paddled over the edge of the drop, and the next and the next... We solved outrageous puzzles of movement and timing - playing speed chess with the water, weaving ourselves completely into the river. We lived for those moments of clarity, when you were totally committed to the line. To that thread of truth. And all those days of friendship and worry and concentration and smiles melted together into the best feeling...

And there was playing until we couldn't hold our paddles, a million skills to learn and millions of things more to do after we learned them: surfing, backsurfing, spinning holes, pirouettes, polish endos, or just zooming around on the water laughing non-stop. I'd never had so damn much fun!

The water is so beautiful – all that power and complexity, all that mystery and unknown. I found myself sitting and watching little eddies, the tiny whirlpools and subtle turbulence. And who wouldn't be mesmerized by an entire river casting itself off a waterfall and pounding into a massive hole? It's a look straight at reality. It's the truth laid out in front of you, sunlight glinting off the spray while the boulders you sit on shake with its power. The question is, do you answer when you hear it calling? How can you turn your back on it?

I got asked by my mentors on more committing trips, and I went. In some ways it was more of the same, but with the greater commitment came new territory. The places got more spectacular, and more dangerous. More importantly, the trips changed their tenor. I found it was one thing doing first descents near home, whether it was class five on steep creeks or big water. Even on the most remote runs, at least you weren't far from people. But doing it up in the wilderness of Canada, Alaska, the jungle, or farther away still, was another thing altogether. The pure fun of zipping a clean line becomes less the point, and something else steps in. The moves might be similar, but a new set of emotions becomes important when you're out in the middle of nowhere, deep in the bottom of some canyon, alone with a friend or two. You look up at the vertical walls. The river disappears in front of you around a corner, and all you can hear is a roar. Then you know the whole game has changed. I call it the real shit. Lots of people, even experienced paddlers, don't necessarily like it. But some people do. You start paying attention to different things when you're totally committed.

Every sense comes alive. Your awareness heightens in every way. The water is your life, and you see and sense everything about it. You listen to yourself and your partner and there's no bullshit. You stretch yourself out and there's no dividing line between you and the beautiful, dangerous place you're in. Every decision you make has huge consequences and so you treat it with care, with a delicacy and intensity that puts you entirely in that moment. The smallest details become immense. Each surge of the current, each paddlestroke, each word has an importance beyond what it could ever have in any other place. And for those minutes, hours, or days, you become a different kind of person.

At some point over the years, I realized that for me kayaking was no longer a sport, it was much more. The decisions I made out there gave me something I needed. I needed the water and its beauty, its power and subtleties, its challenge and inspiration. I needed the friendships it had helped me make. I trained like mad, concentrated on every skill I could, and committed myself to my judgment. The harder the trip and the more it stretched us, the more humbled and small I felt. And the happier. It was like seeing a little farther into a special world. Sharing something beyond friendship with the people I went with.

The point isn't that you fling yourself into huge drops and monster holes, it's that you learn to live each moment with care and skill.

I have a lot to thank my friends for, not just their help in approaching class five, but what it means. They taught me how to look at more than the hard whitewater. That it was a privilege to be in those spectacular places. How important it was to respect and meet the river on its own terms. And never to lose sight of the fact that it is bigger than you in every way. Most of my best friends are people I've spent those times with. I can't separate them out of the feeling of approaching the horizonline. Friendship is a part of class five too.

I've messed up and been hurt. In 15 years of class five paddling, I've had three serious accidents. I dislocated my shoulder the first year I was paddling, right in the middle of a long class five rapid. My paddle hung up on a rock and I didn't let go. Luckily, I was able to roll and get to the side. My friends reduced the shoulder there on the talus with a foot in the side and a couple of yanks. A good lesson that lasted for 13 years of healthy paddling. But sometimes you forget even the best lessons. I had a lousy season two years ago. Maybe I wasn't in as good shape. Maybe I was distracted. Maybe my time was up. First, I hit an underwater ledge at the bottom of a 50+ foot waterfall. I had scouted the thing carefully, even swimming below to check the pool. It looked okay. Shallow, but manageable. The approach and lip of the falls had some weird things going on, but I ran it exactly the way I thought it should be run. It was a full on car wreck at the bottom. Concussion, tweaked ribs and a lesson I thought I already knew: sometimes you can take care of everything you see, and still not take care of everything. Later in the year, a moment's inattention left me plastered upsidedown at high speed on the front of a boulder. Separated shoulder, crunched ribs, dislocated collarbone, and more. It was led off by a decision like thousands of others I've made, but which had very different consequences this time. Sometimes an accident isn't caused by an outright mistake. Sometimes, it's the consequence of a perfectly reasonable decision. The instant in which I made that decision and the moment's lapse equaled a year of rehab. And it could have easily been a lot worse. So reality's there. I've checked it out some. In the end it'll keep you honest no matter who you are.

Other very strange things have happened that could only be put in the "shit happens" category. I try to keep in mind that people can get killed by the shit that happens.

If you seriously go looking for your limits, then eventually you'll find them, but you might not like what happens there. The obnoxious thing is, you might not even realize you're there until it's too late. We get away with a lot because water is almost always forgiving. We call that luck. I'm certain that it is possible to get away with more than we realize now, and people will always be plumbing this margin. But the water also does some weird, weird things. You can't always see them no matter how closely you look, or how cautious and skilled you are. I've run lots of rivers and thousands of hard rapids over the last 15 years. Quite a number of them were first descents. I've faced a lot of questions about whether something was runnable or not. I go on a rational analysis of what I see, sometimes it's meticulous. But mostly I go on a kind of deep intuition that comes out of my relationship with the river, my feeling that day, at that minute, on that run. My choices have been carefully made and always spot on - almost. But the more complex the water, the more things can happen. There are several times when I've been broached, pinned, or tangled with submerged logs which could never have been seen no matter how long we scouted. Other, more bizarre things have happened. I've needed help from friends. I've helped them too. I've pulled a couple of corpses out of rivers, which was not enjoyable, but it was a damn good reminder of what might be on the other side of luck.

The most upsetting thing I've ever experienced didn't happen to me. It was watching my best friend go for the worst thrashing you could have and still live. But that was just the start. He lost his boat and was left with the choice of trying to swim through a series of huge ledge holes, or climbing a 500 foot vertical rotten cliff to get out. He climbed. I could do nothing but watch. The scariest thing is being helpless. It's an empty, terrible feeling. It took him a long time to get up, and I decided during that climb that I don't like being a witness. He made it, finally. That was some years ago and we both have scars. I think his are worse than mine, but mine bother me too. After experiences like that you have to ask yourself where to put the balance point. And you've got to realize that sometimes there are things you might not see which turn out to be the point of the whole show. Anyone who treats the river cavalierly is just a little more ignorant than he thinks he is.

I've always pushed to do harder runs, but I consider myself a careful paddler. You've got to balance those tendencies. I've run lots of bizarre rapids across the entire range from steep creeks to big water, and many things things that are extremely intimidating. But I have never run a rapid I was afraid of. On really hard rapids, I make my decision if, as I analyze it, an intuitive feeling of balance and clarity comes over me, a certainly that the moves fit and that I can do them. Sometimes it feels as if I've poured myself right into the river. If I don't find that feeling, then I walk. Every top paddler I know does the same kind of thing, but with his own twist. Some are more analytical than others, some more intuitive. A few are impulsive, but very few. And none of them goes looking for trouble, although some people might think they do. All of them are honest with the water, even though they might have problems in their normal lives. Within my own intuition, I have an ear out for subtle feelings or doubts, and that has saved my life and a friend's life at least once that I know of.

The thought above depends upon having a choice about whether you'll run a rapid or not. Twice, I've been in the first descenter's nightmare: far in the wilderness, walled out with no portage possible, and having to run what looked like a fatal rapid. These situations were caused by decisions made long before reaching the actual rapid. They are the only times I've ever headed into something that I actually didn't think I could run, but simply had no choice but to try. I can only assure you that you feel pretty damn small at that moment, and pretty damn lucky afterwards. Both turned out, neither was pretty. You never know exactly what you are up against, no matter how experienced you are. No knowledge can ever substitute for taking the step into the unknown. Maybe when all is said and done, those rapids weren't as hard as they looked. All I know is each one looked really, really bad from the one place where you could scout. And in facing that question about the unknown, you find yourself climbing over a lot of emotional topography and asking a lot of questions. You think pretty hard about what led you into that situation and what it might mean.

I've seen people get a lot of different things from the river and from class five. It's all in what you bring to it. If you go looking for challenge or for mystery, you'll find them. Treat it like a snowboard in a halfpipe and that's what it will be. If it's for chest thumping, bragging rights, getting scared, looking for a rush, celebrating friendships, being cool - it can give all these too. I guess I feel that it's such an incredible gift it should be used well. I think most people who stick around know how much it can be, whether or not they put it into words. It's the greatest balance of fun, seriousness, and truth I've ever found.

There are some other lessons too. Most class V from 25 years ago is class four now, or even less. We've upped the ante a lot, as we kept looking for the edge. Disregarding all the grays about ratings, really, the way we use the term it just means whatever the edge of runnability is at a given time. Each time we do another harder river, nip off another portage, find a steeper run, go for a higher water level, that's water under the bridge. Pretty quickly, we look for something higher, bigger, faster, or weirder. We change, and the class five changes. We never stop exploring, both it and ourselves. So to me class five is also a word for a special kind of learning. It says, "push hard, but remember – what you do in the next few seconds means everything." That means class five is a physical rapid, with a beginning and an end. But it is also everything the physical place touches inside you, all the ripples of meaning it has for you, and those things will go on for the rest of your life.

Class five is about your limits. What you can control, what you can come to with a steady, clear mind. Those limits change within you, from hour to hour, or minute to minute, even on a single run. They change with equipment and experience. They change from person to person, and year to year. Some of the guys in my generation may already be getting too old and stiff to keep pushing the edge of class five. They've been there, done that, and now they have families and other concerns. But even if we continue, there's already a new set of people who will try to take it past anything we ever thought possible. And when these new guys push as far as they can, the next generation after them will already be hungry for more. You pass a baton and then step out of the way. I think though, over time they'll all probably be asking the same questions that we did, because the river has the power to say certain things.

And take my word for it, there's always some pretty wild stuff going on. There are guys out there looking for the real shit. You just don't hear about a lot of it because it stays where it matters most - between a few close friends and the river.

Whenever you enter the game, whatever door you come through, that's what you accept as your base. If you've got the desire to find answers, the river will have the questions. So I always keep in mind that no matter how hard we push, there is no end and there are no final limits. The river will always have more.

***

With thanks to the rivers I know, and my partners.

The Lure of Numbers: River-rating as Art and Artifice

<u>Author's note</u> – these ideas have had a series of reincarnations for me. From the 1980s through the early 1990s, as I was repeatedly faced with pushing runs that did not fit the current rating system, I made notes about the problems. I came to believe that the rating system was in essence, a short-hand theory of how we described and interacted with rivers. It was dependent on past experience, and had to be flexible enough to incorporate new experiences, including new techniques, different kinds of rivers, regional differences in features, new boat designs, and especially new understandings of what is possible. Most of all, we had to realize it would be forced to change when our vision of what was possible on the river changed.

These things led in about 1993 to my writing up a detailed proposal for a different rating system and sending it out to about 50 paddlers for vetting. However, even before I sent it out I had deep misgivings, because in the process of thinking about the ideas, I came to believe that we couldn't describe enough in any system to make up for people's limited experience. A short-hand description could not and should not ever be more than a sketch, and precision wasn't possible. Further, I was convinced that the only thing we needed to do was open the top grade and leave everything else in place, so we didn't cram all new hard runs into the same old Class V forever.

I don't believe in the mechanical use of ratings. Thinking something "is only class IV" can easily blind people to what is actually on the river. A river is one place you should never be too rigid, and definitely should never take along too many preconceptions. Likewise, I've seen enough weird things happen on rivers to know that we can't rate something like danger very well because our imaginations never plumb the complexity of what water can do. Horrendous looking drops can be safe, and simple, innocent situations can hide hideous things. Well-known paddler Corran Addision recently nearly died (fall of 2008) when he got stuffed under a steel girder hidden in the backwash of a benign-looking hole. Others have had similar experiences.

However, after my proposal went out, over the next few years others went on to make specific suggestions that were based on parts of the ideas I set out, or on their own experiences. Those included organizations like American Whitewater, and individuals like Corran Addison (the "Addison System"), guidebook authors (Grant Amaral, *Idaho Whitewater*; Andy Embeck - *Alaska Whitewater*), and others. In about 1997 or so, I was invited by *Paddler* magazine to do a point-counterpoint with Addison and his proposal, and shortly thereafter I wrote up this essay for *River* magazine. Basically, I repudiated my original proposal, even though it had some interesting ideas.

So here is the essay essentially as it appeared in *River*. I list the kinds of suggestions people had proposed, but only to knock them down. The simple truth is, many important facts about dealing with rivers cannot be incorporated into a rating system. So overall, this is an argument for simplicity, with an explicit respect for how complicated rivers can be.

I argue for the art we derive through experience and against the artifice of numbers and complex rating schemes. As Einstein said of scientific theories, "they should be as simple as possible, but no simpler."

***

If you think about it, one of the stranger things we do in our culture is to specify every aspect of our lives in terms of numbers. We've got digital clocks, speed limits and - for god's sake - minimum daily requirements for every vitamin and trace element identified by science. There are part numbers for the chip that controls the timing in your Toyota's fuel injector, and hundreds of psychological tests that supposedly describe your personality, intelligence, and self-esteem. Computers ensure that everything about you will eventually be bar-coded or encrypted into long strings of zeros and ones. If you like numbers, western culture in the new millennium is a very good place to be. And given all these, I guess it's inevitable that we also would try to stick numbers on even the most changeable and ephemeral part of our world – flowing water.

The sport of river running has grown rapidly over the past 20 years, with equipment and attitudes changing along with the knowledge of what can be survived. As each generation comes along with its own challenges and ideas, the ways that we look at rivers and rapids evolve. This holds for the pleasures we seek on the river as well as for our views of difficulty.

In kayaking and rafting, our measure of difficulty is the river rating scale. It has done yeoman's service the last 30 or so years but has lagged behind the changes in the sport, and is beginning, at least in some people's minds, to show a little wear around the edges. It is a deceptively simple system, just a number from one to six that characterizes whitewater in terms of the difficulty you might expect if you try to run it. Class I is flat moving water, while Class II includes waves and rocks and requires some maneuvering. As one moves up through class III and IV, each step involves a large increase in difficulty and a coincident development of skills, until at Class IV+, the rapids you are dealing with are complex and often powerful. They require advanced maneuvering and a certain roll on both sides. A distinct jump then gets you to Class V, which in many ways is the outpost of the scale. These rapids nearly always need to be scouted, are at the upper end of difficulty, and involve possible injury or death. Even though only a relatively small number of kayakers run Class V, the main problems of the rating scale reside there.

These nice descriptions sound very reasonable, as if we've encapsulated some important truths in a few words, but they fall flat when compared to the complexity of a real river. Novices often look at this rating system like it is magic and it usually takes years before a paddler uses the ratings with confidence. Even then, that confidence may only apply to the first few grades and the kinds of runs common in their region, which leads to confusion because the numbers don't seem to generalize very well to different rivers, either because of size or the types of features, or just the history of local paddling. Ratings of difficult runs beyond the novices' experience sometime seem to evoke a sense of mystery and they look to the numbers to tell them the answers, like numerologists and astrologers divining some deep secret truth. They compare this rapid to that one, this run to that run, but there is nothing mechanical about it, because the nuances are all hidden in experience.

So the novice might ask a simple but profound question of this scale: how do entire rivers fit into these numbers? The honest answer is that they don't. The ratings can say quite a lot to you if you know how to listen and <u>don't</u> expect too much. But it takes years of experience to know those tricks of the trade, because in the end, the impossible job of any such rating is using a static number to describe a complex and changing reality. Within this paradox lie the art and the artifice of river rating.

When we speak of an art, we normally think of a skill that is intuitive, nurtured by long practice into a deep, fluid, and spontaneous understanding. It is a word that we generally reserve for mature painters, sculptors, or musicians. In contrast, an artifice is a clever trick, strategy, or device that accomplishes some goal, such as a stage setting for a play that is so well crafted it gives the appearance of reality.

The art in river rating comes from experience and allows you to read the important subtleties of a river in a simple number. In contrast, the artifice in rating is the clever trick of capturing the river within that number, or perhaps a set of numbers and symbols. Clearly the person interested in art would prefer to develop his intuition through experience, although this is an uncertain struggle that will take many years. The one interested in artifice would like to construct a more complete rating, hoping that he can capture some of the intuition of the expert and communicate it to others. I confess that I tried very hard for some years to do that, but failed.

The upper end of difficulty is where the problems lie. For the life of the old scale an odd taboo has existed which reserves Class VI for "unrun" rapids. By this logic, as soon as a rapid is run it is down-rated to Class V. As ever more difficult rivers are run, an ever larger range of rapids are stuffed into this grade. As a result, the Class V rating contains a bizarre mixture of different types of rapids which range drastically in difficulty and danger, because the many innovations leading to harder runs have been compressed into this single grade. Clearly, if you are a little out of sync with the ratings, you may get in over your head by mistaking somebody else's rating of Class V for your own.

At present, there is a huge difference between "easy" and "hard" Class V. In fact, within this one class a highly experienced kayaker probably includes a range of rapids equivalent to the difference in the entire rest of the scale from Class I to Class IV. If this seems far-fetched, that is because the rapids done over the last 6 or 8 years are astonishing and include such things as huge waterfalls, intimidating long sequences of large drops, banking and ricocheting lines through congested chutes, and big water lines into long series of exploding waves and closeout holes. Needless to say, the general consensus is that if you make a mistake while doing such rapids, you probably will die. And although you might think that Darwinian selection would eventually put an end to this foolishness, there are those who thrive on it and seek to push it further. So far, they show no signs of slowing down.

Since people are not going to quit doing harder runs, the solution to the down-rating is simple and generally agreed on. Obviously, the taboo of using Class VI needs to be rejected. One can use Class VI, VII or beyond, add plus or minus marks (V-, V+), or use a decimal system like that in climbing with ratings starting at 5.0, 5.1, 5.2, and going as high as needed. Either gives room for the sport to grow and puts no limit on ratings of difficulty. All these types of ratings are in use now. The key in all of this is the tremendous amount of experience it takes to appreciate what the ratings can tell us. Essentially, it requires many years of experience across many types of rivers and creeks

A fundamental problem comes in describing the types of rapids included in Class V. There are quite a variety, each requiring distinct skills which largely depend on the size and steepness of the river, and the particular kinds of features. Kayakers usually consider flow levels and gradient essential information. The reason is because these form a natural separation in the type of skills needed.

Examples might be a steep creek with 300 cubic feet per second and 200 feet per mile, or a big river with 20,000cfs and 30 fpm. For the cognoscenti these numbers go a surprisingly long way in specifying the kind of rapids you can expect, especially if they know the kinds of bedrock peculiar to the area. However, for those with less experience things are not so clear, and so an additional menagerie of descriptions is often tagged on: tight chutes, bedrock waterslides, congested boulder drops, pourovers, keeper holes, boily eddylines, exotic boofs, and so on. There are even references to regional characteristics of classic runs, such as "Sierra type," which refers to the peculiar weathering of the granite bedrock, the slides and scouring, punchbowl falls, boulder-choked rapids, and the kinds of gradient seen throughout that spectacular mountain range.

The distinction between types of skills centers around proactive and reactive techniques. On steep creeks and small rivers, the paddler's experience is typically built on dealing with water features smaller than his kayak and current that he can overpower. Here, he needs more aggressive techniques such as those stressed by slalom: precise forward and turning strokes, greater boat speed, planing the boat over drops, and keeping the bow up. In contrast, on bigger rivers the size of the features he is dealing with are much larger than his kayak, the current so powerful and the speed so great that he cannot overcome them. Here he is forced to use more reactive techniques: using the water's speed to position himself, "getting small" to penetrate waves, dynamically balancing as he rebounds off turbulent cells and holes or maintains balance on powerful eddylines. It is possible to include these types of variables in a rating, adding a distinction between steep creek to big water, and by implication, the skills required. At least, it might be possible if you believe that the rating can capture the experience.

A further variable that has been included in one or more of the rating systems is danger. It has some intuitive appeal, at least at first glance. Surely running a rapid with a runout into flatwater is less dangerous than one above a 200-foot waterfall. Likewise, running a complex line with possibilities of vertically pinning or wrapping on a log is definitely more dangerous than the same line if it is clean. The difficulty can be the same, but the danger is very different because of the consequences of an error. The problem is this: is a class III move above a deadly strainer captured by the grade alone?

While rating danger has intuitive appeal, it disappoints when you consider it carefully. The problem is that you never know how close to oblivion you actually are, and fear of some possible consequence isn't the same thing as knowing what will actually happen. Another way to say this is, difficulty rates our experience, while danger rates our imagination. It should be apparent that some people have much more active imaginations than others. And it is a simple fact that much of the time the river has other things in mind than what we imagine.

Other variables sometimes considered are portages, the length of the run, weather, temperature of the water (e.g., with glacial rivers), and how far it is to help. A case can be made for each one, however it is obvious that as more variables are added, the ratings get cumbersome. They turn into mere descriptions of the runs. The practical problem is how much information can be distilled into a system and how much should be left up to the experience of the river runner.

In the early 1990s I constructed a rating system includeing most of these variables, applied it to about 20 difficult runs of all kinds, and pried reactions out of 50 or more paddling buddies. The rivers included classic steep creeks, "cutting edge" runs with multiple portages that might someday be run, big water expedition runs, and also some bizarre runs like the Santa Domingo in Mexico that didn't fit the current ratings at all. In 1993 we had done the first descent of that river, and had been faced with class V+ cascades as well as long sequences of huge travertine waterfalls in a deep jungle gorge. I also included several other runs, such as the Shumulja in Mexico, where we had essentially canyoneered a river in a deep gorge, and followed it underground. The inventive use of extensive ropework combined with difficult paddling was clearly some that could be applied generally to rivers that were currently considered unrunnable. I used it to illustrate where the sport was likely to go and how the current ratings were limited.

The people who looked at the proposal were from six countries, primarily top kayakers, but also included rafters and a group of intermediate kayakers. The reactions were fascinating. The intermediates, and especially the people who were starting to work into Class V, couldn't get enough information. The longer, more elaborate and intricate the ratings, the more they liked them.

In contrast, the most experienced paddlers insisted that no amount of detail in the ratings actually told you what the river was like. Some of them were downright bad-tempered in their opinions, with the gist of the reactions best expressed in the old saying, "there's no substitute for experience." Perhaps most interesting, they actually enjoyed leaving doubt so that they could discover what lay between the lines. In effect, the ambiguity and confusion of the old rating system were virtues, because their pleasure in running rivers came from finding their own answers. They didn't want a new and better system, because they knew the art hidden in the old.

The reactions show that certain things we look for on a river will never be fit into a rating no matter how clever or complete the system is. They show that the artifice of the system may blind the newcomer to the art of the river.

All the give and take highlighted some other gems hidden within the old rating system. For example, its spareness forces you to realize the core of kayaking is coming to your own personal balance with the river. It denies assertions that a rapid can have a precise difficulty and character, and instead, tells you to make your own decisions and trust your own judgment. Much of the joy in kayaking lies in taking personal responsibility for each moment you flow with the water, and this holds true anywhere, on any river.

So next time you consider the rating system, don't believe that a single number or any combination of numbers can tell you what you really want to know. You have to go and experience the river itself. There is no other answer. After all, numbers are only numbers, and artifice can never substitute for art.

***

Artificial Whitewater and the Meaning of Rivers

Over the past few years, the creation of several dozen whitewater parks has opened up a peculiar situation in kayaking. Not everybody feels this by any means, but some of us who were brought to rivers by the lure of natural beauty now feel uneasy about the collision of two opposing goals – the original ethic of experiencing the natural world versus driving a bulldozer into the river to make it do what we want.

Originally, many of us went to the outdoors to experience a greater world where human concerns were small and nature spoke with its true voice. Probably nowhere else can people experience so directly one of the powers that shaped the world, than while kayaking a wild river. Our ideal was to adapt ourselves to the river, learning its language and following its path.

In contrast, there has been a concerted movement among whitewater aficionados and economic developers to create play-waves, rapids, and as of last year, even entire circular whitewater rivers run by pumps. The goal here is different; it is to maximize our fun by changing the river – or even fully creating an artificial river – to suit our desires. There are many arguments pro and con. Some assert these changes will bring kayaking tourists to the mountain towns, or fill a need in places where there is no river or whitewater. The places help people hone their skills and introduce a huge number of spectators to a sport they'd otherwise never see. Plus, if we have the power to do it, why not maximize our fun?

I don't want you to get the impression I hate these kinds of things. Actually, I was doing this on a smaller scale years ago in the 1980s. In what used to be a mucked out irrigation canal, I spent a lot of time freezing my butt, building eddies using wire mesh cages and piling rocks, rolling boulders half the size of a sofa, and stringing wire to hold slalom gates. I even built a surf wave by maneuvering large chunks of cement, and some of my own ready mix to solidify the piles at low water. I did a lot of it at night to avoid scrutiny.

For a number of years when the water rose, I had a nice little slalom practice site and just downstream a little surf wave with perfect eddies to cartwheel and squirt in on either side. Gradually with winter's thick ice prying things loose and high water shoving anything movable downstream, nature dismantled my work.

Another case is the creation of a great playspot, Brennan's wave here in Missoula, named after Brennan Guth, a friend, excellent paddler, and widely liked hometown boy who died on a river in Chile several years ago. For as long as I remember, there was an old broken weir just downstream of the Higgins bridge with rebar sticking out of it. Originally put in place by the Orchard Homes Ditch Company in the 1920s to maintain flow into their ditch, it crumbled over the years, leaving a dangerous hazard. However, high water gave a glimpse of what was possible. The crumbling pile of cement and rebar created a sticky, violent, dynamic hole, but without a good eddy. I was the only person who played in it for years, although I know Brennan and a German friend did later in the 1990s. The place was a handful. You also had the nice thought that just underwater lay that rebar, as chunks of the weir with twisted rods of ¾ inch steel were littered downstream. I lobbied hard in about 1987 to replace it with a designed feature that would give the Ditch company their head and also make a non-lethal playspot. The city's redevelopment department thought it was a great idea, but the time wasn't right. There were too few paddlers in town to make any difference, the fishermen didn't want anybody touching the river, crumbling weir or not, and the Ditch company treated me like I was insane. This same project finally was pushed through as Brennan's Wave two years ago, 18 years after the first attempt. The difference was a combination of private backing, patience by the several people trying to see it through, 50 times as many kayakers, development of the riverfront park system in Missoula, and the motivation of honoring Brennan after his death.

Whether we like it or not, rivers change. And whether we build spots to honor friends, create competition arenas, or just to have fun, the questions remain. For the 1996 Olympics, the dewatered part of the Ocoee River was redesigned and made into a slalom course. The thought went, "It's a dead river so why not make it useful?" It occurred to me at the time that this is exactly the argument people make about salvage logging after a fire. The trees are dead, why not use them? If you accept the one, it is hard to argue against the other, suggesting we should be careful about where our choices may lead.

The question is, how does this change our relationship to rivers? How does changing rivers to enhance play features fit with respect to a naturalist ethic? How does the will to control the river itself fit with our desire to be challenged?

I'm not taking sides, because I see there is value in both and exchange across them. Clearly, my past efforts show the same compromises. I think it's worth considering the problems and implications.

Like all of its adventure sport cousins, whitewater kayaking began with a sense of loving the outdoors, being close to nature, and for some of us, the enticement of being in places that were huge, empty, and beautiful. The goal, often unspoken in our youthful minds, was to experience mountains and rivers on their own terms, and we relished the confrontation of cold and struggle, and sought to live within powers that were far beyond us.

It was always taken for granted by dam builders, miners, and engineers that one could – and should – shape the natural world like clay to do the bidding of humans. Natural resources were there to be used, and it was a sin to leave them lying in the ground, or in the case of rivers, flowing in their natural course, when we could make use of them to run a power plant or store irrigation water for parched farmland.

It's curious that this mindset has made an end-run around our Earth Days and Green sensibilities to embrace the excavators, cement, and backhoes in the river. It's no longer to make electricity or grow things that people eat, it's just to have fun. Surely we have undertaken this with less entitlement and more sensitivity to the land, and we're not asking to put entire rivers in pipes, dewater a riverbed, or flood a hundred square miles of land with a dam. But in sport after sport the same thing is happening and nobody has taken a step back to ask what it might mean. Features that we used to go to in order to escape the artificiality of a city and its asphalt, concrete and fluorescent lights, now are being recreated artificially by our own hands for our own purposes. Is the six feet of space around us on a surf wave or in a hole the only thing that matters? Isn't that a bit self-centered?

We're in the early adolescence of what might be done. Perhaps the biggest quandary that juts its face into the scene, is what confronts me when I think about going to Brennan's Wave. Brennan was my friend, but I'm not so sure he'd have spent much time at his namesake. He paddled all over the world, eagerly going places for new and different challenges. I'm certain he would have liked a good playspot to hone skills, work out, or enjoy a session five minutes from his house. I am equally sure that he, as somebody who was philosophically minded, would be asking questions. Where will this lead? Perhaps to a renaissance in the number of people who will enjoy and value free flowing rivers. Or, to a distraction, where those who like the convenience but lack the desire to escape into the real nature, stay in the city and leave the wilderness to others. Maybe it won't lead anywhere. Only a few dozen dedicated paddlers seem to frequent Brennan's wave, despite it's being there 24/7. When the Lochsa is in, there are even fewer.

I don't have any great answers, and sometimes I think the questions don't even matter. I went out one time last spring to Brennan's wave. I'd passed over the bridge while on an errand, looked down at the river as I was driving by, and saw the usual hole had been transformed by the high runoff into a long set of beautiful waves. It was raining, nobody was out, and it struck me that after 25 years of paddling on it and decades of living by it, the river was showing a side of itself that I'd never seen.

I went home and got a boat. I was rusty, but ferried out to the center wave. It was four feet high and 40 feet across, a beautiful, big surging green animal, and I spent the next several hours cutting back and forth, spinning, backsurfing, and carving. It was quickly clear why nobody else was out. At this high flow, the other paddlers couldn't surf any of the waves in their tiny playboats because they weren't fast enough. I had it all to myself.

The bridge was almost directly above me, and downtown just a block away. It was rush hour with cars passing, honking, sirens going, people walking, but out there on the water I was in another world. The river silenced it all. The last sunlight came through a break in the clouds, showing a rainbow over my shoulder. I sat there in the boily eddy behind the little island, and the blackbirds wrestled in the dripping willow bushes right over my head, trilling in the final sunlight. The swallows dove right over the top of the wave, circling up high and swooping down to shoot past me just off the water.

I thought about Brennan. If he were still alive, he'd have been right there beside me, just like it used to be - the only ones out at twilight as it started to rain again. In the sounds of the rushing water and the blackbirds' song, I could almost hear him talking about this artificial wave, Brennan's Wave, a little embarrassed it was named after him but happy it was here. In my mind, he and I talked about the problems with artificial whitewater. I don't remember all he said, but I remember his meaning. Maybe we made the spot, maybe the excavators set all those boulders down to create a ledge, but this wave was as real and as beautiful as anything could possibly be. The river took what was artificial and transformed it into living water. There was no paradox. All that was necessary was the right frame of mind and the flowing river.

***

Section Two: Bigger Issues

The Cutting Edge- Part 1: A Beautiful Anarchy

I recently had a discussion with some passionate steep creekers about the "cutting edge." They love their pastime in the way only wonderfully fanatical kayakers can and insisted that steep creeking was the "the most cutting edge" in kayaking — the area with the highest level of difficulty and people pushing limits the most. I disagreed with them.

The cutting edge is usually defined as the hardest things done in the sport. This sounds impressive and dramatic. It also implies something that cuts like the sharpest knife. The truth is more complicated.

When you start looking at it, the cutting edge is hard to characterize because it refers to so many different things. It has a media-induced buzz, but it is also used as slang for people's ideals, including what they are struggling toward and what they think they have accomplished. It represents these and much more — from the most neurotic of our desires to the precious things we aspire to, which sometimes are one and the same.

The cutting edge is a huge, sprawling confusion — more like a crate full of broken bottles than the edge of the single sharpest knife. There isn't just one edge, there are lots of them, with people throwing more in all the time. Like a piece of broken glass, the edge changes constantly and drastically from one aspect of the sport to another. There is no measure of the edge, although we attempt to put numbers on it — the height of a falls, the flow in cubic feet per second, the feet per mile, and our ever-elastic rating of Class V. In all of these, the assumption is that the higher the falls, the bigger and steeper the river, then the harder and more cutting edge it is. However, anybody who has been around the sport for a good length of time will, if pushed, be able to list provisos for all of these. It depends on the nature of the drops, how clean they are, what support is possible, the equipment used, subtleties of the line, how much you know about a run, objective hazards, and many other things. Finally, even though it is implied as "razor sharp," many parts of the cutting edge turn out not to have much cut to them.

In terms of difficulty, I would argue that every aspect of the sport has its cutting-edge element, because people are always pushing each thing as far as they can take it at any given time. People are constantly defining new branches of the sport, so the ways in which you can be at "the edge" are always multiplying. Consequently, there are many dozens or even hundreds of cutting edges. Yet, we only recognize certain things.

Let's start with some things that probably everybody will agree are currently cutting edge.

An example I saw just yesterday would be the Young Gun Productions crew. By name and action, they and their many followers are certain that what they're doing is raddest and baddest cutting edge, which includes 100-foot waterfalls, hard steep runs, hard play moves, their self-chosen name, and their movies (*Young Guns*, *The Source*, etc). Their ads say they are doing the highest waterfalls, "new heights" in freestyle, and "global first descents" in "impossible locations." Despite the hyperbole, my hat is off to them — there is no doubt they are great kayakers and paddling very difficult whitewater.

A contrasting example is that this spring a small, two-person Austrian-Brit team quietly dropped into the last unrun section of the Indus Gorge and kayaked it. This is challenging big water in a canyon that is steep, cliffed out, and forbidding. It helped that they were alpinists as well as excellent paddlers, which made the rope work and complex portaging more feasible. That extra set of skills was another dimension that had to be integrated into the paddling skills. They went on to do the first descent of another river coming off 26,600-foot Nanga Parbat into the Indus that had an astronomical gradient, and which they described as having "more sieves than eddies." My hat is off to them, too. There is no doubt that this is a huge accomplishment in the expedition world.

Depending on your point of view, perhaps the Indus runs are more cutting edge than the Young Guns. Or, if you're partial to the youngsters, you may think that their "big-air" freestyle moves, waterfalls, trips to Vietnam and Africa, and steep Sierra drops are more impressive. Comparing these two current examples starts to underscore the variation in what people consider cutting edge. As a simple fact, the more things you look at, the less clear that edge becomes.

There are a lot of strange things about this appeal to the cutting edge. For example, tune in next year and people will have done even higher highest waterfalls, soared to newer heights in freestyle, and done more global first descents in even more impossible locations. You can see the problem. If the location was "impossible" then by definition they couldn't be there. If what they will be doing next year will be so earthshaking, does that mean they're slacking it this year? Is the cutting edge nothing more than a synonym for what's new and cool?

The edge is often used as advertising shtick and easily degrades into clichés and hype. Guinness got cold feet on world record waterfalls shortly after the initial widely publicized efforts of one paddler led to a quick succession of other people running higher falls. It's unclear why anybody was talking about world records in the first place, but now, this quest has taken other forms, with a group supposedly "testing the limits of free fall." I'm left with a quizzical look: What does it mean to test the limits of free fall in a kayak (150 or so feet) when, for example, BASE jumpers go off things from 400 to several thousand feet, and for that matter, skydivers regularly do free falls from 15,000 feet. To complicate matters, a skydiver even went out of a plane at 10,000 feet in a kayak, doing flips and rolls on his way down. Hilarious, interesting, and let's face it, very weird. Why is a free fall in a kayak so important? We appear to be talking about the skill in landing safely when running a large waterfall, but did the skydiver in the kayak have less skill than it takes to run a 100-footer clean? Is this getting ridiculous? Funner? Both?

In search of clarity, let's look at the opposite extreme and restrict it just to kayaking for a minute. With all the breathlessness that accompanies the new feats, you might note that sometimes people do things that stand for a long time and are unrepeated, like Walt Blackadar's amazing 1971 solo of the Alsek. Such things are undisputed examples of cutting edge. The fact they aren't repeated looks like it is due to the runs being so hard and exposed that others do not want to take them on — cutting edges that stand the test of time. That might be so. However, again there's more to it.

I firmly believe that anything one paddler does can be done by many other current paddlers. Nobody is so good that he can do things no other paddler can. This is a myth about the cutting edge. What is really happening is that people of multiple talents and equivalent ability make individual choices about what challenges to take on. The sport doesn't just constantly progress by the best people pushing the same limits harder and farther. The edge has all the quirks of the people who seek it.

The sheer variety reflects how different rivers and creeks can be, how many ways they can be difficult. Not only that, it reflects how differently people can see these things. Frankly, it's anarchy out there — people pick their own challenges, and most of the paddlers aren't interested in trying to repeat something that has already been done. They deliberately do things that are new and different. They want to put their own mark on the board with their own style. The cutting edge is a combination of all the things people do. It shifts and changes according to interest, equipment, focus, publicity, time, sponsorship, and even fads. Most of all, it reflects the huge range of personality and what individuals see as their personal challenges.

Consider waterfalls again: The focus on running big waterfalls has led to it as defining cutting edge in many people's eyes, particularly non-paddlers. Paddlers have gone higher and higher, and even claimed world records. But arguments about the details sprout up just as fast: whether something was 98.5 feet or 100 feet, whether that is higher or lower than 32 meters, whether it was entirely a freefall, or whether putting jugs of water in the bow of the boat (to help keep the nose down) should be counted against the run, or even whether running the same falls at a different water level makes it 1.5 feet lower or higher. The little arguments multiply like mushrooms. Every single such comment illustrates the edge is not a single thing, but more like a generic symbol. We seek absolutes — the hardest, the highest — but only can ever find what is relative. The details shift and differ, making the edge a strange and fuzzy place.

Particularly over the past 10 years, big gnarly falls have taken a special place in some people's minds. The appeal is straightforward — a big waterfall is impressive. Height speaks for itself and is immediately equated to difficulty: the higher the falls, the more difficult it must be. On an aesthetic level, the visual simplicity leads to great photos that anybody can look at and say "Wow!" You can communicate the feeling of difficulty instantly at a gut level. In contrast, if you've ever given a slide show, you'll know it's hard for viewers to understand what is going on even in super difficult Class VI + whitewater. After a certain point, everything is white and chaotic, and it doesn't matter if it gets whiter and more chaotic. Thousands of rapids are harder and more dangerous than probably any waterfall that has been run, at least in the sense of requiring more moves, more energy and skill to do them right, and having much worse consequences for failure. By way of proof, let me ask this simple question: How many people have died in hard rapid, and how many have died doing big waterfalls? The score, to state it in a very crude way, is about 100 to 0. No excellent paddler has ever died doing a high waterfall, but plenty of top-end paddlers have died running hard rapids. Now don't get me wrong — more deaths doesn't make kayaking hard rapids better; every single one of them is a tragedy. My point is simply this: Using death as the ultimate measure of difficulty and consequences, waterfalls are far less dangerous than the usual Class V. However, the finality of that single arc off the edge is spellbinding to non-kayakers and kayakers alike, so waterfalls take a special place at the cutting edge.

If you think a little further, running waterfalls is a rather odd pastime. Surely it is spectacular, which for most people is probably a good enough reason to do it. However, I'm reminded of the oddness by the guy who ran a 105-footer in Oregon in an inner tube after "scouting" for three minutes. The kayaker who ran the falls originally scoped it out for months, but the tuber just glanced at the falls, climbed aboard, and shoved off. He made it fine, although he fell off his tube at the bottom. That means he ran the falls as well as several well-known paddlers ran their big ones. But it begs a question for the present discussion: What does it mean that something formidable in a kayak is easy in an inner tube? Why is it that a waterfall requiring cutting-edge skill and daring in a specialized kayak can be run by somebody using a tube you can buy for $10 at a gas station? If you think about that very much, it suggests running falls in a kayak is silly. At least it undermines making such a big deal about height. What would happen if the goofy, skilled, and ballsy tuber did 107-foot Alexandra Falls in the Northwest Territories? How would we make sense of such a run?

We may never know because it's doubtful that the tuber will get sponsorship from Goodyear Tires to roam the world running huge waterfalls in his inner tube. You will never see the inner tubing equivalent of *Twitch* or *Source*. Maybe he can get hooked up with the team that is supposedly testing the limits of freefall. However, just imagine what would happen if he were shown running even one of the things they do, much less the showcase 107-footer right after the kayakers. It'd make the whole thing into a joke — the edge-daring kayakers against Zoltan the Spoofer. Further, a high school friend of mine — a highly skilled gymnast, rock climber, and kayaker — jumped off a 180-foot waterfall, landed perfectly, and survived. A little worse for wear, but okay. That's 70 feet higher than the kayakers are looking at. And Al Faucet ran a 100-footer, Sunset Falls in Washington State, in a wooden dugout canoe nearly 80 years ago. People have gone over 160 foot Niagara Falls in barrels. Why is it a big deal to run a smaller falls in a kayak than it is using an inner tube, a dugout canoe, a barrel, or by jumping?

There's no question kayaking requires more skill, or at least different skills than tubing or jumping, but a question arises: Isn't it weird to celebrate kayaking skill when that skill isn't actually required? We seem to be making something harder than it really is. The edge should lead us to a greater understanding of our true limits, not to deluding ourselves about our skill and daring. When the inner tubers are seeing more clearly than we are, then we've got a problem. We need to apply the old Chinese proverb: "He who criticizes me correctly is my teacher." The question for us collectively is, are we willing to learn from a tuber?

Waterfalls are an example of the peculiar and loose definition of cutting edge. They are spectacular. Some of them are hard and dangerous; others are dramatic and high but easy in an inner tube. You'd think that if the edge was so sharp, it would at least pop the tube.

Let's go back to that original comment about steep creeking being "the most cutting edge" in kayaking, and then consider contrasts between the types of edge paddling. What is different and why?

Expeditions put a premium on doing difficult things self-contained out in the remote sticks. It's not only the difficult paddling, it's everything about the difficulty of where you are. The first time a proud steep creeker does an expedition in a Third World country where he gets strung out puking with some GI problem and still has to do Class V for the next week, he probably will change his tune. There's a different element of mental and physical toughness involved. Or, if he does one of the big wilderness rivers up north, camping out of a boat for days that weighs 80 or 100 pounds, running hard, big water, portaging, living on slim rations, he probably will come back thinking that creeking on day runs with an unloaded boat — no matter how hard — is not the sum of the sport, and actually is a lot funner and less obnoxious than other forms of the edge. But this can immediately be reversed. When the creekers' boats are unloaded, they can take bigger risks, and attempt wild moves that you would never try in a loaded boat 100 miles deep in the Himalaya. This turns the tables. The expeditionist taken down a cutting-edge creek will not be dissing the creekers afterward. Any of the rest of us will be in the same situation if we proclaim our favorite runs are the hardest of all terrain.

To complicate things, the cutting edge of steep creeks hybridizes with other forms. Here is a personal example: I soloed the full Clark Fork Yellowstone Canyon in one day back in 1994. It's basically a steep, Sierra-like river in a deep granite canyon, rated Class V+/VI, 26 miles long, and about 3,000-plus feet of drop. It has never been done without portages, and if you go there you'll see why (Jackson, Wyoming, paddler Greg Goodyear did it once with an astonishing four portages). I had a flow of about 2,000 cfs (considered high) and did eight portages (considered low), all of them strenuous, several while roped, and quite awkward around cliffs. There are no big waterfalls but there are lots of steep, long rapids and sieves. The Class V does not let up till the last couple of miles, which are continuous Class IV. I suppose this shows if you can list enough numbers, the run must be cutting edge. It is a spectacular place, going from alpine meadows at the put-in to a deep desert canyon at the take-out. Usually, it is done as a long two- or three-day run. I didn't know the run (I had run it once five years before), and that was part of the draw for me. I was looking for a full expedition-like experience on a complex run, all condensed into one day. I put in at 6 a.m. and took out at twilight, utterly exhausted. That's approximately three major steep creek runs in a row — runs you don't know — in the wilderness, with portaging complexities, severe exposure, and no support. It's a multi-day, hybrid wilderness/steep creek/expedition run, done solo in a day. Tommy Hilleke and John Grace's one-day descent of the Middle Kings in 2007 is somewhat in the same vein.

One could say this kind of thing was cutting edge, but actually it's a specific personal challenge, and only a certain kind of person would want to do it. Hilleke and Grace's run was also in remembrance of their close partner Daniel DeLavergne, who had died the preceding year. Suffice it to say, there aren't a lot of people out there seeking these particular edges, a fact that doesn't mean they are better or cooler or harder. They fall somewhere between steep creeking, hard river-running, and expeditioning, making them strange to characterize.

People haven't repeated either of the above runs in the same ways, but it isn't because they can't. More likely, it is because there's no reason to do it except the personal reward one finds for having taken on these particular challenges. Others attempt to go faster, or add new sections, do it at higher water levels, and so on. Despite all the numbers above, the runs are not quantifiable in the sense of a "world record" waterfall. They're just hard. Try one of them and then we can talk about it. The paddlers running 100-plus-foot waterfalls could say the same thing to those of us who haven't run something over 60 feet — or whatever our personal limit is.

Here are a few additional examples, some of which are variations on a theme:

- Scott Lindgren's runs of the Upper Karnali and Tsangpo.
- Olaf Obsommer's multiple steep runs in Norway; his descents in Greenland and the Indus in Pakistan.
- Felix Lemmler's "exponential" runs on the Oetz and waterfalls up to 42 meters (137 feet).
- Willie Kern's amazing runs in the Sierras, and recently in Tibet and China.
- The "Triple Crown" trip that Gerry Moffat put together in 1998, where we did the three classic northern big-water ex-pedition runs — Sustina, Alsek, and Stikine — back-to-back-to-back. (which Erik Boomer and Tristan MacLauran did them-selves two years ago).
- Hilleke, DeLavergne, Grace, and company accomplished their "Seven Rivers" expedition as another extension —

doing seven multi-day Sierra classics in one summer (2004). The same group also did something I find especially impressive — the 60-mile Stikine Grand Canyon in a single day.

There are many other paddlers doing many other things that could easily be on this list, including the "Young Guns."

The crux is, people want to define their own challenge. That's what the edge is, for each of us personally and for the sport as a collective.

There are plenty of other things. Ben Friberg started pushing the idea of a vertical mile of creeking in a single day. Interestingly, we did something similar back in the late 1980s and early 1990s on the North Fork Payette —three runs in a day (a vertical mile). That metamorphosed, and in 1993 I did 8,500 vertical feet of Class V in a day. In 2007 the group of Bryan Fletcher, Fred Coriell, and Ryan Casey did a full 10,000-plus feet (two vertical miles) — six top-to-bottoms in a single day. That's incredible! Friberg is encouraging creekers to do this, but they have different terrain — smaller volume, steeper, tighter drops, more "technical" in a number of senses. So which is harder — multiple top-to-bottoms back-to-back-to-back on the NF Payette, or multiple runs on a steep creek of your choice? There is no answer to that because they are different kinds of paddling.

Which is the cutting edge? Well, I guess both might be, in their own strange ways. Finally, consider Steve Fisher's runs of various huge, wild cascades in Quebec. Are they impressive enough as single runs, or will he have to do a vertical mile of them to be cutting edge? It seems safe to say they stand solidly by themselves.

The bigger issue for the cutting edge is, across the sport there is no reason at all why Blackadar's, Hilleke's, Lindgren's, Friberg's, Fisher's, the Young Gunners', mine, or anybody else's challenge should be the yardstick for the cutting edge. These multiple examples — all different and all difficult — show there isn't and can't be any clearly defined edge that everybody agrees on. That's not the way the sport functions for people on a personal level, and it doesn't reflect how the sport progresses.

I can only speak accurately about the things I've directly experienced, but another prospect for "most cutting edge" would be if you saw what the North Fork Payette looked like at 6,500-7,000 cfs. It more or less qualifies as a steep creek, but with a massive amount of water. No waterfalls, but lots of steep drops. The drops are not sieve-like, or bedrock slides, or waterfall cascades, but incredibly powerful and fast, big water — 30-mph exploding waves and holes going solid for a half mile or mile at a time. It's full-on balls-to-the-wall. The half-mile stretch through Jacob's Ladder/Golf Course is maybe 250 fpm, but with 6,500 cfs – 10 to 20 times the usual "creek" flow. I challenge any kayaking aficionado to take a look at that river at that level and then tell me waterfalls, creeks, or even expeditions are the single "most cutting edge" part of kayaking. T'ain't so. You will have to make room for more.

Big water has its own cutting edge, and I think nearly every paddler would have to completely reappraise his attitude once he dealt with certain rivers — even those that have been run before. Devil's Canyon on the Susitna at 25,000-plus will never be a pushover. The Stikine at any level. The Tsangpo, Indus, Oetz at high water, Thule Bheri in Nepal, the Zambezi at 90,000 cfs, as Fisher recently did, and so forth.

In the end, what it means is that together we have made an astounding sport with enough challenges to satisfy all of us for a lifetime. We're generating new challenges all the time. We hold in our hands a diamond in which we are constantly creating new facets — a gemstone that becomes more beautiful and ornate, with ever more edges the longer we work it.

Height doesn't define the cutting edge, or steepness, flow, or total vertical. Nobody owns the cutting edge, and nobody can say what is hardest. Not the Young Guns — despite what they claim — and not any of the rest of us — despite what we do or criticize. All of us can create an edge of the sport if we are motivated and skilled enough. The cutting edge is open to our imaginations — expeditionists, waterfallers, creekers alike — and it exists on flowing water that is big and fast, small and steep, and everything in between. There will be new cutting edges next year and the year after despite the old edges not being surpassed or even repeated, and even if the edges don't cut very much.

The cutting edge is a symbol. In its anarchy it represents what is new, hard, and interesting. It represents fads, boat design, and advertizing shtick. It represents the ideals we strive for, and the places we go for challenges. In all these senses, it is a microcosm of everything from the neurotic weirdness to the most beautiful aspirations of our sport. What more could we ask for?

***

The Cutting Edge in Kayaking: Part 2 – From Difficulty to Gifts

Introduction

My original essay "The Cutting Edge in Kayaking" ran in the July 2008 issue of *American Whitewater* magazine. Tyler Bradt, an outstanding young kayaker who last year ran 107-foot Alexandra Falls, responded to my original article with what he called "a rampage beyond the cutting edge", which redirected the topic. He offered a defense of big waterfalls as a legitimate and beautiful part of kayaking, feeling that I had demeaned them in my first essay. He coupled that with comments on the state of the industry, its current demise, and suggested that technical innovations and sponsorship of his compatriots of Young Gun Productions (YGP), would revive the sport into a 100 million dollar Industry. For the magazine, and with Bradt's permission, I contacted about 20 top people across the sport and asked them for comments on the two essays, and to offer their own visions of where the sport has been and where it might go.

If you are interested in that complex set of responses, look on the *American Whitewater* website. It includes essays by Jim Snyder, Corran Addison, Eric Jackson, Shane Benedict, Joe Pulliam, Risa Shimoda, Aaron Pruzan, Landis Arnold, Jamie McEwan, and three top younger kayakers: Patrick Camblin, Nick Turner, Austin Rathman. However, they diverge too far from my original topic to be included in this book, although the second part of the essay below makes passing reference to several of their points. For example, my essay said nothing about the financial past and future of the sport, or about why companies should (or should not) sponsor young athletes, or whether we might design specialized kayaks to do big waterfalls, or about cost-benefit tradeoffs between dollars spent on athletes versus molds for boats, or whether the sport is driven by professionals pursuing the cutting edge, or by everyday paddlers pursuing their own personal enjoyment. I also didn't talk about family and beautiful experiences on the rivers (brought up by several of the commentators) because I've written extensively about them else-where. Had those been my themes, I would have written a different essay that wouldn't have been on the idea of the cutting edge.

My primary purpose in the first part was to examine what the "cutting edge" might be, and I focused primarily on the idea of difficulty. This second part was being written at the same time, as it included some important ideas cut from the first essay, and also focused on something different that is key to the entire show – the personal cutting edge. As the first essay argues, the cutting edge is so diverse because it is driven by people's personal feelings about challenge. This idea applies to everybody at every level of the sport, no matter what kind of kayaking they do, and is not something that only the hardest of the hardcores grapple with. In fact, it may be just another way of talking about what makes our sport so great – it offers so many different challenges that it can be everything to everybody, no matter what our level.

The cutting edge is usually used to refer to the hardest things we do, but it actually is just slang or a buzzword that hides more than it describes. If there is an edge, it is not a single edge, but more like a crate of broken bottles — hundreds or even thousands of different edges, some sharp and dangerous, others dull, some spectacular, and others less so. It represents all the things we do in the sport that are new, interesting, fun, and different. Contrary to what the words cutting edge literally suggest, some of the edges actually don't cut at all, but seem relatively benign. The edge is incredibly diverse. It evolves in unpredictable ways. It is essentially driven by individuals' personal challenges and desires, and their own creativity in applying their skills to a challenge that they find unique and personally interesting. It's an expression of who they are and what they seek. Most people aren't really interested in doing the same things better or higher or faster, although that sometimes is part of the change. Much more so, the edge is a symbol of freedom. It is anarchy as opposed to some constant, predictable expansion along clear dimensions. There aren't any clear limits to it, except that we could be sure people will continue to figure out new cutting edges as experience, equipment, designs, skills, and attitudes continue to change, which they always will.

I described a number of specific examples of what people might consider the edge to be. I deliberately contrasted the different branches of the sport: steep creeks with big water, expeditions, hybrid runs, waterfalls, peak flows, doing multi-day runs in a single day, and so forth. The intent was to show that every branch has its cutting-edge aspect that will stretch or even go beyond the edge of aficionados of the other branches. If you are great at one, then the tables are turned if you go into another branch. The point was, no part is "better" than the others. Another point was, nobody is so good at one branch that there are not plenty of others who could do the same things. Some humility is in order.

Additionally, I didn't get into freestyle or competition because the article was already way too long. I cut out the drafted sections on those, and for the same reason, cut sections on the importance of building on earlier people's experience, and on equipment and designs — even though it is obvious many of the things we do can't be done without specialized boat designs. The edge is all mixed up with changes and innovations in equipment. The best paddler in the world couldn't flat spin an old Dancer or a 13-foot slalom boat; shorter boats make different runs possible; every design that makes one type of move easier also compromises other maneuvers.

I took special aim at waterfalls because they seem an exemplar of many peculiar notions and confusions about the cutting edge. They truly can be difficult and look spectacular, yet people seem to believe in a simple equation that higher is better and harder. Falls have been a centerpiece for the cutting edge for the last 10 years or more and have generated a lot of press, especially the claims about "world records." Among other things, I pointed out that an inner tuber had run a falls as high as the current "world record" and asked what that meant — if anything. It's clear that more skill is involved in running a 100-footer safely in a kayak, and there's no question that a kayak is infinitely more versatile for running rivers in general. But what are we to make of this crazy dude doing our "world record" in a $10 tube? Do we dismiss him and blithely go on, certain that our sport is so great we don't have to pay attention? Or do we ask ourselves with some humility whether we really are doing something special with our "world records?" Do we ask how "cutting" the edge really is if it's not even sharp enough to pop the dude's tube? And who's to say he isn't having as much fun as us, or that it isn't harder than what we do? In a list at the end of the article, I added that a Swiss paddler had already broken the current world record by 30 feet – apparently unknown by the guys who think they are the current record holders – which again begs the question of what is so important about free-falling in a kayak. It certainly can be an incredible experience. It certainly is part of the cutting edge, but just what does that mean? People need to answer that question for themselves.

My larger message was that these questions apply to everything we do. No aspect of kayaking is better than any other. They all have their cutting edges, and it's all great fun. Those edges have evolved with the sport, and they evolve for each of us personally. It's silly to get on a high horse and think we're so special that the tubers don't have something to show us. Simpler can be fun too. Huck Finn didn't have any less an adventure down the Mississippi because he was on a wooden raft instead of paddling a state-of-the-art plastic kayak. Talking about some apocryphal edge hides more than it illuminates.

I also would like to add that when waterfalls lead to front-page claims of world records, it is a notion that seems completely contrary to what rivers are and what they teach. A primary lesson rivers teach is endless change, and of our inability to hold and grasp flowing water. Our sport is defined by taking part in that ever-changing flow and learning to live with endless change, at least for a short time. We all know a river's character varies drastically from instant to instant — water levels are up and down, eddies surge, waves build and break. It's what makes running rivers so difficult, challenging, and fun. Our skills don't capture the change; they allow us to meld with and become a part of it. That's a grand and inspiring experience: literally being change and evolving with each paddle stroke and rapid. At the same time, rivers have a lesson of timelessness; they flow through the eons, and when we join them for a few hours or days, they allow us a glimpse of that timelessness. There is nothing constant, except perhaps the realization that we are much, much smaller and more finite than they are. They have been here millions of years before us, and will continue to flow for millions of years after we're gone. We don't change them. They change us. So to claim one has captured something valuable in a precise number, and that there can be a "world record" of 98.5 feet or 107 feet, seems silly and self-centered to me. It seems to contradict the lessons of change, timelessness, and humbleness in the face of the infinite. This is doubly so when the height of the falls is so small. The example of the Hail-Mary tuber, this dude in an absurd floating toy, seemed to call out these things in a humorous way.

But the waterfallers should take heart because they are not the only ones who need to look over their shoulders. The inner tubers are ready to filch other precious kayaking treasures. While I originally focused on the twist of a tuber running a big waterfall, a friend told me this same guy has run the entire Class V stretch of the Futaleufu and a host of other gnarly rapids. Are the Alsek and Stikine next? Maybe the expedition paddlers will be in the same position as the waterfallers soon. Maybe we're all "misunderestimating" the lessons here. Eric Jackson got it. After he read my and Tyler's essays, he wrote to say that his company had already sponsored two tubers and given them a private jet.

In case you don't know, there also is much greater precedence for doing massive and dangerous big water in an inner tube. When American rafter Ken Warren attempted to be the first to descend the Yangtze River in 1986, the Chinese had several teams "racing" him. They were made up of workers from various cities that belonged to athletic clubs; most had no river experience at all. However, Chinese nationalism spoke strongly to them, and they didn't want some foreigner to be the first to run their great river, a river that symbolized their history and culture. From a polite standpoint, they used what was essentially a big rubber inner tube, or capsule, into which they would strap themselves. They ran some incredible rapids this way — including Tiger Leaping Gorge, a massive stretch of whitewater that is stunning in its raw violence and immensity. Let me put it this way — you won't see anybody running it in a kayak anytime soon. They paid for their daring, as at least six of the 15 team members died over the course of the failed several-thousand-mile journey. The craft would get caught in an apartment-building-sized hole, and the river would brutally slam and spike them for minutes at a time until eventually they were torn out of their harnesses. As the loose bodies flailed around inside the careening capsule, the hatch would be wrenched open by the water, and people would disappear into oblivion.

If any of us, including the Young Guns, had to face that high a chance of dying on a single descent, then we almost assuredly wouldn't do it. That's a good thing as far as I'm concerned. It also is a statement that the cutting edge is something different than what most people think.

The fact is, we carefully choose things that are within our skills, and deliberately do not attempt things that seem impossible. The Chinese tubers were truly on the cutting edge — actually they were way past it — and it turns out not to be a place where you can expect to have a long shelf life. As my good friend Bob McDougall aptly said about such things, "There's no future in it." So in light of this, what we're talking about in kayaking most of the time is a sort of well-mannered cutting edge that we're very careful about selecting, while thousands of things are much harder and far beyond our skills, strength, and equipment. The full range of Nature's power and beauty is on display out there. Take a look and compare it to what we do. Personally, that seems inspiring and wondrous at the same time it is humbling. If we could do everything, then we'd probably be looking for another sport. But we can't. In fact, we only do a tiny slice of the possible. The Tsangpo Gorge is a case in point; we have to wait for its absolutely lowest flows to even do parts of it, and still we only sneak down the side chutes of the easiest sections because the center lines are too hard. The inner and lower sections appear unrunnable no matter what the level, and the only alternative route is climbing over a 14,000 foot pass for days. The Stikine above 25,000 cfs is another case, and if you consider that it gets to 70,000 or 80,000 every year, the usual run at 10,000 to 17,000 is pretty feeble in comparison. It just happens to be all we can handle. But we don't need to go that far away, how about Colorado's Yule Creek at peak? The Clark's Fork Yellowstone at 6000 or Smith Creek at 1000 cfs? Neither of those flows are all that much water and they happen every year, so what are we waiting for? Or if we really want a challenge, how about the release flumes on any big dam? Snoqualmie Falls is 270 feet and sitting there plump as pudding for all to see. There's a major highway right to it, a huge spectator's platform and space for a thousand people to watch us run it. Plus, I saw another beautiful 250-foot-high punch-bowl falls the other day, and then looked through a set of impressive photos of falls ranging from 200 to 1,000 feet high. There must be tens of thousands of waterfalls in the world that are higher than 107 feet. If we put our heads together, we could make a very long list of such things. An endless list. So we won't be running out of edges for a long, long time. The question is, do we only look at what we can do, or do we also remind ourselves of what else is out there in the real world? Both, I hope. The first is our drive and optimism, the second is our humility and perspective. Together they balance into a sense of inspiration and in the end, into awe.

A sobering twist on the cutting edge is revealed by when and where deaths occur in kayaking. Tellingly, there are almost no deaths on the highest-end whitewater. Essentially nobody dies attempting horrendously difficult rapids or falls. Nearly all the accidents occur in strange and even bizarre situations on standard runs that are well within the kayakers' abilities, rather than on runs where the best guys are hanging it out. We point at the most dramatic things as if they define the edge, when really that isn't the part that cuts. The edge that truly cuts and kills lies in the subtleties hidden in the water, in the undramatic things that don't catch our attention, that lurk unseen beyond our awareness, and that injure or kill us or our partners on runs we believe we know. In this sense the edge is hidden and unknown and cuts hardest and deepest when we least expect it. We take care of all the dramatic things just fine, and then die in a rapid we know well, or due to an unknowable hazard or an inexplicable mistake in an otherwise normal river situation. Conrad Fourney, Rich Weiss, Pablo Perez, Tim Gavin, Dugal Bremner, Chuck Kern, the list could go on and on, and it makes me deeply sad to think about each one. These accidents underscore in a different way that the cutting edge is nothing like what most people think. It doesn't exist where they point, and many of the things they believe about it simply aren't true.

I don't want to minimize the deaths, but the numbers also tell this story: that kayaking even at the highest level is fairly safe. Very few people die. If we truly were facing a readily identified edge that cut, then you wouldn't see this. In contrast, the first ascent of the Himalayan peak Nanga Parbat shows the opposite. Before Hermann Buhl climbed it in the early 1950s, the various German teams had lost more than 40 climbers and sherpas. Forty deaths to climb one peak. It sounds insane to me. The same has been true on other Himalayan mountains. On one especially unlucky day, 11 climbers died in a storm on K2, including some of the best mountaineers in the world. A similar tragedy occurred just earlier this year on the same peak. Other similar tragedies have happened on Everest.

Such things never have occurred in kayaking. We've never seen a team of five kayakers all die in the middle of a big run, although I know of two possible candidates for something vaguely similar. One team that came the closest was filmed on the flood-stage Sultan River in Washington State. The footage appeared in Lunch Video Magazine's issue 16. Purely by happenstance they filmed a violent landslide 100 yards upstream that obliterated the rapid they had just run and filled the canyon with a colossal slumgullion of match-sticked trees and muck, damming the entire river. If it had happened a few minutes earlier when they were in the rapid, at least three or four of them would have died. This is entirely equivalent to an avalanche on a mountain — except it is so incredibly rare on the river. The total surprise and astonishment they expressed just underscores that even though water crashing through rapids seems chaotic and constantly dangerous, canyon walls do not collapse on kayakers as often as avalanches bury climbers.

The other example occurred on the Clarks Fork of the Yellowstone in Wyoming, where a team of seven paddlers somehow followed each other, one after the other, into a horrendous sieve. The river drops a good 50 feet through a pile of broken, car-sized blocks with gnarled root balls littered throughout, then into another steep, messy cascade and another sieve and then over a nasty 25 foot waterfall (this is the same incident described in my story *Reflections on Danger and Certain Death*). One died, two were trapped in caves and if they hadn't been rescued by a team following close behind, probably would have drowned. Three were seriously injured with broken bones. The astonishing thing is that only one person died. However, the point is, just like the landslide on the Sultan, the utter bizarreness of this story underscores how infrequently such scenes occur in kayaking.

This may mean that the cutting edge in kayaking isn't all that cutting. But frankly, who the hell would want it to be? Maybe it shows we're way more careful. Some people might say it's because we're so good. But maybe our edge is milquetoast in comparison. Maybe the climbers of that earlier era were totally nuts and accepted an astronomically higher possibility of death than we do. Maybe the inherent uncertainty of control and cascading power in whitewater paradoxically leads us to take fewer outrageous chances. Any realistic appraisal would also note that the terrain and hazards are different as well. Himalayan peaks have far more "objective hazards" than even really hard kayaking runs. On a big peak you can easily get killed by avalanches. Weather, high winds, and storms are all constant major concerns. Rockfall, shifting glaciers, and seracs go with the territory. Almost never are any of these present in kayaking. Considering the comparison between kayaking and Himalayan climbing, one thing is for certain — there's not as much cut in the cutting edge of kayaking. Or, at least the way we approach it tends to dull that edge considerably. That should be considered a mark of sanity. It's bad enough as it is to lose a friend; it would be insane if it were worse. Yet, as you are about to see, that depends on how deaths occur and what they mean to people.

In the 1980s before the fall of the Soviet Union, western paddlers were stunned by the announcement that Russian rafters and kayakers were doing "class seven." It seemed impossible — how could they be paddling something two grades harder than what we were doing? Reportedly, dozens of them were dying, so it seemed that indeed, they must be way out there. After some exchange, however, a very different reality appeared.

It turned out that river-running was one of the few things the communist regime didn't get around to restricting, and all the passion, freedom, nationalism, brotherhood, camaraderie, and deep sense of individual heroism that we know so well, blossomed in a riot in that microcosm. They were starved of these things in their normal life, and the river released it all. They weren't doing anything that was harder than the usual Class V, but they were using the damnedest, lousiest, most jury-rigged craft and absurd gear cobbled from anything they could get — hazmat suits, aircraft aluminum, inner tubes(!), and anything they could find to construct a floating vessel that could be piloted down wilderness rivers. What they were doing was Class IV and V, but they were doing it in the most dangerous ways, with horribly poor gear, where injury and death were possible on every trip — and yet they relished it. They sought the ultimate challenge and found things that all of us reach for — freedom and the power to control our destiny — and to them that cutting edge was worth their lives. "Living is the only thing worth dying for" is a trite slogan for us since we have near-infinite freedom: but it was absolutely true for the repressed people of a communist regime who found free-flowing rivers as the outlet for their deepest feelings and their desire to choose how they wished to live — and to die. Their cutting edge was their freedom. As one of them put it, death on a river was not just acceptable, it was to be revered. It was "a glorious way to die." Certainly it was better than being a depressed alcoholic hiding in a bottle of vodka and numbing oneself to a dismal world, unable to affect one's fate. They were heroes to their companions and renowned in their groups. Plaques were erected on the rivers, toasts made. Great stories told and retold. They were like the knights and heroes of the Old Days, of myth and legend.

This leads directly to my own personal ideals of the cutting edge. There are two of them, and they are entirely opposite in some ways. The first involves difficulty. It is the desire to pull together the entire repertoire of skills on a single run or even in a single rapid. In retrospect, it's what I did on a number of my favorite runs. For me, an ideal cutting edge run is one that requires paddling at the highest level on big, steep rivers with every kind of feature, thus demanding from the paddler every kind of technique from big water to slalom to freestyle, just to do the rapids. That is a different definition of a "line" when you have to pull all the stops and every skill out of your quiver. Then, it includes portaging and rope work. In a sense, it is combining the entire sport into a single run, or perhaps even a single rapid.

Each individual aspect of kayaking has a cutting edge, but the more interesting thing to me is putting all of the different edges together. In this light, the Young Guns are making great strides. Also, I greatly respect what Steve Fisher has been doing because he shows this with flair. Scott Lindgren's expeditions show this as well. The crew of Daniel Delavergne, Tommy Hilleke, John Grace, and friends provide other examples. Olaf

Obsommer's teams likewise. There are other superb kayakers doing their own versions of it.

Reinhold Messner, in his book *The Seventh Grade*, proposed that the style of a climb, its boldness and risk, should included in the assessment of how hard it was graded. The above is my seventh grade. When you can take all the skills that we collectively have as kayakers, learn them, excel at them, and then find a run where all of them are needed in order to do it, that's my ideal. Finally, for me personally, the step after that was to do the same thing, the most technically demanding and diverse multi-day runs, but solo.

This leads into my mirror image of cutting edge, which is the purely personal aspect of any run and doesn't necessarily have anything to do with difficulty. It is something open to anybody who ever puts on a river. It is the personal evolution that comes from melding with a river, feeling its change as a part of you. That might be a sense of wonder, beauty, and friendship on an easy float with no whitewater at all. Or, it might be the fun shared with a beginner who goes down his or her first Class II run. I remember the feeling of personal freedom and sheer joy, of new possibilities unfolding, and it's a wonderful thing to share that with somebody else. It is not an edge that cuts, but one that gives life and shared warmth.

On the serious end of this edge, I'm interested in the personal crucible where I seek something much deeper. As a long-time martial artist, I treat running rivers as a martial art in the sense of working with nature as the ultimate master, learning to flow with the water from its simplest forms to its most chaotic and powerful. Doing this forces you to find the heart of the river and blend with it. It leads to realizing you're a small and frail human in the face of the grand forces of nature. That perspective has some of the mythic quality the Russians were so attracted to, and I believe this fundamental feeling is a part of everybody's experience. I chose to take it off in a particular direction for myself, seeking long, difficult wilderness runs, and doing them solo.

It is a test of character, a reflection of who you are or what qualities you seek inside.

Every person, regardless of his or her level or expertise, can experience this kind of rich challenge, and likewise experience both mirror images of the edges I describe. A beginning paddler doing his or her first roll in a river finds a cutting edge, where challenge is mixed with pure fun, and success leads to a sense of freedom. A Class I paddler in the first Class II rapid feels this, and so on up the line.

As their skills improve some paddlers require harder and harder runs to find this same feeling. Others come to find the simplicity and beauty of easier runs, and the "edge" comes from the heightened awareness and deeper reflection. It doesn't require big-league Class V – which actually can overwhelm the reflection – it's all about finding a more rewarding personal balance within oneself. So, the scale can range from fun and freedom to a personal crucible, a fun get-together to a sweat-lodge experience, quiet personal reflection to a vision quest.

All these different senses of personal challenge and freedom are shared across the sport: the hardest-core dude may find them on his cutting-edge run or falls, the Russians found them on their "class seven." But the fact is, you don't have to go to the ends of the earth or do something hard. They are all around you all the time. Every one of those experiences, whether in Class I or Class VI, is a beautiful and valuable personal milestone. And the lesson isn't that what we do is so special, it's that the river has so many gifts. Some of them are easier to see in the drama of a hard run, but the magic happens by all the time disguised in the ordinary moments. Look, and you'll find them.

That puts us right back where we should be. We started with claims of the hardest and ended with gratitude for the gifts we are given. We are lucky to have a sport so rich.

***

Soloing and Taboos

There's always been a taboo about paddling alone, and I happen to think it is wrong. Over the years, for many different reasons I've soloed all sorts of runs and have come to deeply enjoy the time I spent paddling by myself. From all this experience, I believe there are a great many reasons the taboo is silly. This problem actually represents a much more general truth that kayaking is tailor-made to confront: to understand your place in the world and to understand what you are actually capable of, you cannot allow yourself to be shackled by other people's taboos.

It may surprise some readers, but I know for a fact that nearly all experienced paddlers have soloed a fair amount, at least on their favorite and familiar runs, at every level from easy to difficult whitewater. However, they usually don't mention it because it is a very personal experience. Perhaps unfortunately, the outcome of this is the taboo remains because the people who don't abide by it do so quietly, personally. However, over the years I have been criticized by a number of my friends, and by others, especially about my more extended solos such as the Sustina and Stikine. I never said anything, but the fact of the matter is, my runs weren't impulsive, and I've thought a great deal about the value they have for me. So finally it seems worth stating why I solo and why the taboo is something that should be questioned.

Perhaps the simplest reason to solo is that it can be hard to find partners, even for your local run or play spot. Going alone becomes a practical decision so you can paddle.

That is how I started. I didn't deliberately go out to solo runs. I worked out by myself a lot, including all the local runs in my area, and just training on the river in town. Because my schedule was strange and because I was more passionate than any of my friends, I ended up going out at night even in the winter with temperatures down to minus 25. I was cautious at first, but it soon became a normal way to paddle. Everybody has had the problem of getting partners who have time schedules and appetites that fit together. For my timing and appetite, it was impossible. When that happens, the choice is either go alone, or don't kayak.

Also, with care and attention, every such experience turned out to be perfectly safe, even if some of the wintry nights were a little dark and cold. I learned faces of the river that I would never have seen otherwise, every one of which was beautiful and fascinating. Things like how and where the ice forms, how much it changes from day to day and how it responds to the temperature. Or subtleties of how the boat moved and how well I could sense the current in the dark. There were many other things: knowing when the animals came out, where the deer, beavers and musk-rats liked to forage and where their favorite spots were. I felt that much closer to the river because my senses of touch, smell, hearing, and sight were magnified. There were no distractions. The river was the only one talking. And it told me things I would never have heard if I weren't alone.

The attitude toward local runs extended to other, harder runs. For many years, nobody from Missoula wanted to paddle the North Fork Payette River, or drive to Icicle Creek and Tumwater Canyon on the Wenatchee, or do out-of-the-way runs like the South Fork of the Clearwater. So, I ended up going to those places by myself, doing multiple runs solo because there wasn't anybody to paddle with, and because once I was there, I wanted to get everything I could out of my time.

So I went soloing first out of practicality, but once there I found much more. I found I could listen closely in ways I never would if a partner were sharing the trip. I began to realize just how much having somebody else along distracted me from what the river was doing. Alone, I noticed features and had feelings that would be overlooked if somebody else were there. It was a long term lesson in replacing ignorance by experience. Gradually, I became very comfortable by myself even in highly exposed, serious surroundings.

The problem of having very limited partners was true even in the Payette area, which has long been a paddler's paradise. Through the 1980s and the early 1990s there were only a relatively small number of people who ran the full North Fork Payette. From that small pool of kayakers, it was often impossible to get anybody to go up for a second run later in the day or in the evening. Actually, this was also the case with easy runs as well. Right here in Missoula, I have always had trouble finding people to do some-thing a little out of the ordinary, like three runs in a day cruising down the wondrously eddy-filled stretch of the Blackfoot River, from the highway crossing at Roundup to 9-Mile Prairie. It's a fantastically varied run and just Class III, so it's not hard – but I could never find a partner who wanted to spend that much time and effort. One run? Yes. Three runs? No. So, I did it by myself.

In the process of all these different approaches – the workouts, the easy whitewater, and the more serious runs – I discovered a wonderful way of relating to rivers.

I'm not a misanthrope. I certainly enjoy my many partners and nearly all of them are life-long friends. Those I've done trips with probably would describe me as a definitive team player because I firmly believe in working together. However, I found I liked being alone on the water. Having partners is an expression of friendship, but it also orients you differently. Other feelings would come up when I was by myself, there were different thoughts and experiences, and the challenges were also different. I followed these into increasingly extended and difficult situations. It reached the point where some of my paddling friends became very worried about my safety and sanity. And they only knew a few of the runs I was doing, because I wasn't telling them what I was running most of the time. I did multi-day solos of Class V+ and VI wilderness runs, steep creeks, exploratories, and high water solos of extremely difficult runs. I did long solos of hard whitewater, like the Clark Fork Yellowstone, collapsing multi-day Class V+ runs, complete with complex portaging, down into a single solo day.

In that process, I spent a lot of time thinking about those experiences and what I liked about them. As a teenager I read Reinhold Messner, older European climbers like Hermann Buhl, Heinrich Harrer, and Ricardo Cassin, and later as I was doing kayak solos, I read various articles by Peter Croft, John Bachar, and other well-known climbing soloists. It was obvious that they were kindred spirits. The sports involved different mediums, but led to similar experiences. Over the years, the experiences became a call from the river and a personal journey.

The reason people always give when they wag their fingers and intone the taboo, is that soloing isn't safe. That may be a fine rule of thumb for most people most of the time, but there are many exceptions and it isn't an absolute. I'm not going to defend soloing as perfectly safe, because it isn't. I'm only saying that we go to the river to get different kinds of experiences, and soloing fits within that.

I think in general it's a good idea to have one or more partners, just like it's sensible to have good equipment you can depend on. However, even the best equipment can break, and I've seen plenty of situations where even the best partner may not be able to help, so in reality things aren't that simple. Claiming they are is factually wrong. So I would ask another question. Do you want to understand your place in the world, or live by taboos that are mostly right but wrong in critical ways? The answer to that has to be a personal one, and it will reflect what each person wants from the sport and life.

My experience is that when you are paddling with somebody else, it is a social experience. But when you're alone, *the river itself is your partner*. Unless you have had such an experience, I can't tell you how deeply that shift in perspective will pierce you. When you are soloing, you are compelled to intimacy with the river and your surroundings. There aren't *any* distractions.

Soloing isn't the next level of the sport, and it isn't something to aspire to. It's a personal decision about how you want to relate to the river. It certainly can be a challenge, but it is primarily a mental one that shows you the ways in which you rely on other people, even if they can't help you physically. That is, it shows where your mental and social weaknesses are and how your confidence is tethered to other people. Fears usually come from these, because being alone is seen as a threat, and the taboo can be an equally unrealistic herd instinct to huddle together, or to rely on other people's judgment and support when it isn't actually needed.

After a decade of pursuing very difficult solos, I realized that seeking harder runs was only a small part of my interest in soloing, and that some of the best experiences I had had were in easy whitewater. So, I define soloing this way: If there are witnesses, then you're not soloing.

You can see from that definition that it has nothing to do with the difficulty of the run, but everything to do with the quality and type of experience. You can solo virtually any time, anywhere, and at any difficulty; it doesn't even have to be whitewater. The critical thing is that you are fully alone. Soloing is what you do when nobody can see you, and ultimately, when nobody even knows where you are. Those are the circumstances when your inner world comes face to face with the outer world without any social filters or crutches. You are cut free to find out who you are.

Soloing is a tool that makes the river into a mirror and allows you to learn things you otherwise cannot know about yourself. This use of soloing is entirely dependent on your attitude.

People can solo at any level and have a great experience. It isn't something that's reserved for certain people, or for hard runs. It depends on what you want to get from your paddling, whether you are out on a lake or on an easy river, or something harder.

Soloing for me is an act of humility. I don't go out thinking I'm going to rip down a river, or that I'm so good that I can handle anything by myself. I go out quietly to seek a place where I blend into a huge and powerful world. I go there to get away from the yammering of the mainstream world and to seek something pure, beyond words, and treasure the experience. Every time I solo, whether it is on a flat river in the day or night, or on a difficult run, I find things that inspire me, that allow me to share a sense of connection to my surroundings, and a feeling of smallness in the face of the world, like being a precious, small candle flame flickering in the most unlikely of places. I think this is a fact about human existence; no matter how close we are to others we still have an unbridgeable gulf between us. The more we share, the less the gap seems, but it is still there. This is a symbol of life and consciousness. It isn't philosophy, it is a fact. Soloing, to me, is an expression and full realization of that.

I soloed on the North Fork Payette a lot in the 1980s through the mid 1990s, including multiple runs. I once did 5 top to bottoms (8500 vertical feet of Class V) in a day, and a portion of that was solo. I also did quite a few hand-paddling solos, which is another step closer to complete intimacy with the river. You do not have the power from a paddle, so you have to be that much more sensitive to your position, angles, your line, and what the water is doing. Once, I hand-paddled three top to bottoms in a day (a vertical mile in a day), the first one which was by myself. There's a feeling of freedom putting on alone, without a paddle at 6 a.m. just as it's getting light. You know nobody else is on the river, and that nobody else would even consider getting on in such circumstances, which creates a surreal feeling. I've had similar feelings many times, where what I'm doing and the place I'm in are so different and strange that it seems like it can't be real. Places like the Chen Cave where the Shumulja River goes under-ground, or the spectacular vistas of the Alsek River, with glaciers damming up the river. The places are so powerful that they put a spell on you even when you are with partners. Just imagine how much more powerful such experiences are when you are alone.

On the morning when I did the three hand-paddling runs, I remember nobody was on the road. It was deserted. The fog gradually lifted, until only little shreds of mist hung over the river. Heading down into Jacob's Ladder, and again at Screaming Left I had this sense of relaxed freedom, this touchstone of calm strength and confidence, while realizing I was doing something that was risky and utterly out of the ordinary from any objective point of view.

I ran quite a few solo runs at high water (4000 – 6000+ cfs) on the North Fork Payette, basically sneaking the runs very early in the morning or near twilight. I didn't want the hassle from friends who thought it was too dangerous, nor was I interested in the notoriety from a wider group. On one, somebody saw me while I was scouting at Jacob's, so by my stricter definition (no witnesses) it really was not a full solo.

If you accept the idea that paddling has to be done in a group, then you really need to examine the assumptions. For example, are three people safer than two? How about four people being safer than three? I would say that the more people there are, the more disconnected from the river they become. That is because they can't help but be distracted – their attention is focused more on each other and less on the water. They simply are not as in tune with their surroundings as they would be if there was a smaller group, or in the extreme, if they were solo.

If you tease through the issues, what you find is that the taboo is quite arbitrary and risks can be quite fluid. While doing something risky is considered dumb by a lot of people, some things are extremely risky but taken completely for granted, like driving on a busy interstate, or even on a normal street at rush hour, while talking on a cell phone or having a enthusiastic discussion with a friend. You have an astronomically greater chance of getting injured or dying in a car wreck than a competent paddler does in an accident on the river. But people readily accept the driving risk because it is part of every day life. However, not many people paddle, and because you have to go out of your way to do it, it seems like a gratuitous, stupid risk because people don't know what the hazards actually are. This taboo arises from ignorance.

I would never argue that it is perfectly sane and rational to take off and do a top-end run solo. I've done many such runs, and believe it is more dangerous in many ways, especially if you are in a remote place. It puts a premium on your ability to stay within yourself and not get into major trouble. Specifically, it makes portaging harder, and in general, it cuts down the number of options you might have if something goes wrong.

However, it's common knowledge among experienced paddlers that in truly hard whitewater nobody can help you anyway. Sometimes that is true even in relatively easy whitewater depending on the configuration of current, bank, or rocks. Walt Blackadar drowned under a river-spanning log in a rapid that was simple but closed in by vertical walls. He was in a party with six other paddlers and nobody could reach him. My friend Conrad Fourney just died on the North Fork Payette. He had trouble in a rapid he'd run hundreds of times, swam in a strange place, and got flagged on an unseen obstruction eight feet from the bank. He was in a party of four, and another party of four came down while his partners were trying to reach him, but nobody could help. All experienced paddlers can multiply such situations, some fatal, some just scary. I'm not arguing that partners don't make you safer because in general they do; I am only stating that things also happen with some frequency where partners are not able to help. In those situations, having partners can create an illusion – a psychological sense of safety, not a factual one. Personally, I think being alone makes it clear you don't have any possible backup, so you approach the whole thing with more focus without the illusion of help. You're on your own. So when people paddle in a group the question is: Does believing in the illusion of help make you safer than knowing there can be no outside help? Is making this illusion into a taboo safer than knowing the ways in which it is untrue?

I'm not looking for rationalizations. What I believe after more than 25 years of paddling is that every accident is the product of specific factors, and by itself soloing affects very few of them. Every accident is causal, but those in it could not see the link of events. Sometimes the events may be predictable, but usually, the critical elements are unseen and unknowable through scouting or any other means except trial and error. They are particular combinations of time and place, split seconds and inches. The water is usually incredibly forgiving and I can recount dozens of situations in which it seemed a severe or fatal accident could have – *should* have – taken place, but the boat came free, the paddler washed through, the log gave way, and after a few shaky laughs, life continued. The truth is always in the details, and the smallest details can sometimes make the difference between life and death.

I've paid close attention to accident reports, and have plenty of situations to mull over from my own experiences and those of partners and friends. A few examples will show that having more people present does not necessarily affect the outcome in any clear way. The specific paddler's skill or judgment is much more often the key factor. We all make mistakes, and usually, regardless of whether we have partners or not, we are the ones who have to get ourselves out of a problem. Obviously, when you're soloing, this fact is taken to another level.

One friend was in a large group, and he scouted a line in a Class V rapid while the others waited in their boats. He directed his friends down a chute on the far right of the drop. With everybody else downstream, he climbed back up to his boat. As he was getting in, he looked up just in time to see a log wash down and disappear from his sight, going right toward the chute. He got a bad feeling and climbed back up to take another look. There it was, right in the line he had directed his friends through, stuck on a corner in perfect position to wedge the next oncoming boat underwater – which would have been him. He portaged. Had he been getting in his boat right as the log went by – a coincidence that he missed by just a few seconds – he would have headed down and who knows how the story would have ended? None of his partners would have been able to help.

Another friend was running a river in New Zealand with several buddies. Entering a rapid, two of them chose different routes on the spur of the moment, my friend eddied out on river right, while his partner eddied out on river left – straight into a sieve and died. Luck of the draw. I'm sure it's no fun getting the short stick, but even drawing the longer one leaves you with some serious questions. It took my friend some years to recover his confidence about his own decisions.

A top woman freestyler drowned at a major competition a few years ago. There was a crowd of great paddlers there, and they were all having so much fun that nobody noticed her disappearing into several big whirlpools below the play spot. She probably was tired, couldn't roll, then swam. It's a classic case where having lots of people – even dozens of world class competitors – and a festive, exciting group actually created a situation where they were less safe because they were all focused on the social party rather than their safety. There was an atmosphere that gave the illusion of safety, when a lethal spot was lurking just downstream.

One point is, safety does not increase with numbers. It depends entirely on what people are paying attention to, starting with the individual paddler him- or herself.

A further and subtler point is, if you look at any accident, you see strange coincidences that all came together for some reason right then. We call it bad luck, but that doesn't mean that chance was involved. It just means that we couldn't foresee or understand all the elements that were in play. Sometimes they are even more subtle than the above, incredibly peculiar and unlikely. You can call it fate, luck, but from where I stand it is merely the sometimes inscrutable complexity of truth. Soloing does little or nothing to affect these coincidences. But it can affect what is possible after they occur. Those are the situations where having a team can sometimes be safer.

The irony is the taboo can lead people to believe that they are safe because they are in a group. That isn't true at all. Accidents can happen to anybody, but it would be more accurate to replace the taboo by a simple statement – *any time you are on the river, whether solo or with a group of any size, your safety is determined by your personal attention, care, and awareness.* The danger increases any time you are distracted.

Beyond danger, there also is an entire aesthetic side to soloing I alluded to above. I'm not going to encourage others to look for it, but it is there, at least for me, and was the biggest reason I continued soloing.

Perhaps the most beautiful experience in kayaking is flow. There isn't any other sport that demands such intimacy with nature, moving in harmony with the power and intricacy of the river, and whitewater kayaking is the preeminent flow sport. When you paddle well, there is the feeling that you are pouring yourself right into and through the water, becoming a part of its living power. Soloing heightens this, because when you are entirely focused on the river, with no distractions at all, you can weave yourself right into the current. Soloing is the open door for understanding how close to the river you can be.

There also is a deep sense of self that comes from being completely responsible for everything. Clearly, when you're solo that responsibility sits on your shoulders alone, rather than being shared among team members. I like being the captain of my ship, feeling the freedom of action and choice. Soloing is just an extension of that.

Few people dwell on the aesthetics of being alone. There is no doubt that you reach a state of hyperawareness about your paddling and the river that is deeply satisfying. I've found one of the greatest experiences is when I can take the hyper-awareness I have during paddling difficult water solo and widen it so it includes the sense of place. I can take the laser focus I feel toward the water, and lift it upward, seeing the starkness of the canyon, the power of the river, the beauty, and my own vulnerability. All of them cut and shine, like a million facets of a diamond you've only barely been aware of. At those moments, there are no arbitrary barriers, no psychological crutches, and no taboos. Only a truth so clear and pure that it is almost unbearable to look at.

Those kinds of feelings are deeply satisfying to me on a personal level. Moving through a dangerous, beautiful landscape for days, as if I am on the moon or a distant galaxy. Cut loose from the world, fully responsible for each movement, woven intimately into the present in all its richness. There is an immediacy and clarity you will get no other way. The only other place I've ever found something even greater is with my wife at the birth of our children.

Soloing creates a deep intimacy with the river. It's alive, and you feel its every gesture and shrug, sense every flexing muscle, hear every word it says. In those moments its language becomes yours. I've stood alone in the most remote canyons listening to the roar of massive rapids, heard boulders rolling along the river bottom, small swirls murmuring, waves in the eddies lapping and speaking. There was nothing else in the world except them. No distractions, just reality in the rawest form possible. Sometimes the rewards you find for taking risks are worth it. It's just a question of what you go looking for – risks, or the truth.

In the end, taboos are just arbitrary social rules. They are illusion. After all, if you're so concerned about safety, then why go on the river in the first place? You might as well stay at home on the couch and put an extra padlock on the door. I'd rather face the danger and beauty of the world on its terms and leave the illusions behind.

I've always found that the most interesting things happen out at the boundaries of what we know and am drawn to those places. I want to see the view, I want to see what is over the ridge. I want to see what is around the next corner. It's a fascination I have, and I think many people are like that. I have seen it in every child I have ever been around. It may even be a core motivation of our species. You don't find out anything important by sitting comfortably in the middle of a safe place with a lot of people around you. That's boring and uninteresting. This is true of science, art, and of life in general. What would happen if we told our children that they couldn't think about the limits of our knowledge? That they should stick with other people because it was dangerous out there alone. They should think like the group, and be safe? What would happen to our medicine, our art, music, and writing, our painting and sculpture? There certainly would be no adventure. And what would have happened if early humans had come to the north coast of Africa and thought things looked too frightening across the water to the north, or across the deserts to the east? Fortunately for all of us, they didn't listen to the naysayers.

The fossil, archeological, and genetic history of human beings strongly converge on a certain story. Our best understanding is that humans moved from Africa throughout the world, across oceans and entire continents, and to me, this is the simplest proof that as a species and as individuals, we look for the boundaries. When we see one it becomes our goal, and when we surmount it, we look toward the next ridge, and beyond. What must it have been like for humans 30,000 years ago to find, extending through the frigid sea, a bridge into an unknown world that stretched unimaginably far beyond the horizon, nearly from one pole to the other? In 1969 as an 11-year old kid, I watched on live TV as Neil Armstrong stepped down off the lunar lander onto the surface of the moon. My one thought was, "*I want to go there*". I saw the early pictures of sulfur volcanoes on the moons of Jupiter, I built and looked through telescopes at star clusters and nebulae, Saturn, the moon, and the sun. I counted sunspots and watched solar flares explode into space. The unknown was beautiful, fascinating, and alluring.

Science and art are all about looking beyond what other people think is safe, and the adventure sports are exactly the same thing. It is interesting that here at the end of one century and the start of the next, so many people are looking for boundary experiences in their recreation, and that what seems like recreation so readily becomes much more than that. In some ways, adventure sports are the focus of many of those feelings, and I think that is because people can physically work toward identifiable boundaries and beyond them to specific goals. They may feel frightened looking at a rapid or a mountain, but these are physical, knowable things that can be confronted. The goals of the sports are the physical representation of our boundaries – physical, mental, and emotional.

For that reason, certain parts of the sports are inviolate. I set them aside to protect them and to keep them beautiful and pure.

I never aspired to solo; it just came to be something that seemed natural and necessary for the way I felt about rivers and myself. It is like the zen saying that if you look for it, you cannot find it. If you look to solo as a deliberate method that will give you certain things, you will not find them. But if it is on your path and it comes of itself as the next step, then you will take that step and follow where it leads.

I am not a church-goer or a believer of any religion. I'm trained as a scientist and find my inspiration in the natural world. In mountains and rivers, in animals and people. However, I believe strongly in spirituality, our sense of mystery in confronting the things we cannot comprehend. There are limits to science and the rational answers we can find in this world, so I consider it a fact that there are many things beyond my understanding.

But I believe that if you could stand before God and ask Him for a key to unlock the Truth, a key that would allow you to go where Truth was laid out before you, then I am sure that one of the many paths he might set you on would be a huge river that ran through the wilds of the north country, from the ragged high mountains through lonely glaciers and deep canyons, around terrifying blind corners and roaring rapids, and into sunsets that expanded to the infinite horizon. He would put you there alone on the Alsek River at sunset, looking across the Lowell Glacier and huge peaks bathed in alpineglow to make you feel small and frail. He would put you on the scoured black walls of the Stikine, holding on in the rain with rocks falling around you, peering ahead into a rapid that had no line, and no end. He would put you at the brink of a waterfall and not allow you to see the bottom – with no place to scout, no place to portage, no options. He wouldn't ask you a question or give you any advice, He would just lay Truth in front of you to deal with as best you could. And your job, given that key, would be to find the Truth and make it a part of you.

Soloing is a gift.

***

Reflections on Danger and Certain Death

Every paddler knows the feeling of a near miss - the sense that the edge was right there and he or she came Oh-So-Close to Entering the Great Beyond. It might have only been in class II when you were beginning, or it may have occurred in serious Class IV or V when you were an experienced paddler. You all know the feeling: "My god, I almost died right there."

The problem is, most of the time we can't tell what the outcome might have been. There are very few deaths in white-water kayaking, which suggests that usually, no matter how bad it looked or seemed at the time, everything would have been just fine. I will admit though, sometimes it is hard to get away from the feeling of being on the brink of disaster.

One time a highly experienced friend of mine misjudged a tricky move in a long rapid and got flipped. He missed two roll attempts as his paddle hit rocks, and ended up getting washed up high on the pillow in front of a big boulder. The only safe line was to the right, to the left was a short channel ending in an ugly rock sieve. He rolled up, saw where he was, and got shoved left.

His boat fell into a frothing caldron with no exit. Sharp edges of rocks poked up like teeth around the boat as it violently cartwheeled and smashed on them. After the fourth or fifth time his head and shoulders pummeled against them, he gave up. "I got a direct hit right between my shoulder blades. It stunned me and I didn't have anything left. The only thing I felt was a deep sorrow for my wife…" Suddenly, as if in slow motion, the bow jammed upright and he looked straight at his two partners, standing there with wide eyes only 15 feet away in the huge talus boulders, throw-rope at ready. A light clicked on and he began to fight again. Three more cartwheels, a huge shove from the current, and the boat wedged between two rocks right at the edge of the caldron. His friends quickly secured it and he gingerly worked his way out. The three of them stood there in silence for a long, long time, looking at where he almost died.

If we were to boil down all the questions we have about whitewater and kayaking, past all the questions about fun and beauty, about excitement and challenge, right down to the single thing that was most critical, that question might be, "will I die if I mess up and have to swim that rapid?" Death is the very last thing any of us have on our minds as we head out to paddle. The problem is, there is never any guarantee of what might happen.

Our ratings of rapids sometimes attempt to get at the problem of danger and difficulty. Class V is generally taken to mean that a rapid is difficult and that we will face likely serious injury or death if we make a mistake in it. The danger generally goes up with the difficulty. The problem is that our whitewater ratings are such a rough sketch of what the river is doing. While it makes intuitive sense for us to try and include estimates of danger more explicitly, if you start actually trying to apply that idea things get complicated quickly. For example, how do you weigh different kinds of dangers? If you miss a move like my friend did, is the possibility of vertically pinning equally danger-ous to that posed by a log that you can wrap on, or, say, getting swept into a rock sieve or even over a 200-foot waterfall? How can you weigh the possibilities? Are cold water and continuous rapids more dangerous than undercuts or broaching rocks? But even moreso if you think about it, the biggest problem in rating danger is that we are trying to rate what we don't know and only think might happen. Difficulty rates what we have done, while danger rates what we imagine. Another way to say this is that difficulty rates our *experience* while danger rates *imagination*. Since some people are able to imagine the most outrageous things, while others can't see a guillotine even when it's right in front of them, it's not at all clear how that will help us under-stand what the future may hold.

This has some big implications for our understanding of what is going on out there in the river. While everybody can look at a slow Class I river and agree there is no danger, consider the other end where we are *sure* that we know what will happen because it seems so bad and so obvious. With that, we're back to the problem I started with - at some point all of us have had the sinking, terrible feeling that we were very close to oblivion, but when it comes down to it, no matter how strong our impressions we don't know what would have happened.

Things that look safe can actually be highly dangerous in certain situations, while things that look dangerous can actually be perfectly safe. You can even make that paradox into a credo: "the one thing that is certain is that we don't know what is certain." And so that leads us to a situation that at first glance you'd think would be easy to agree on - assessing the difficulty and danger of a rapid that obviously looks like Certain Death.

Consider one of the great Class V runs in the United States, the Clark's Fork of the Yellowstone River, a beautiful 30 mile stretch in Wyoming just east of Yellowstone Park. The river comes off the Beartooth Plateau and cuts down through a deep granite gorge, with mile upon mile of excellent Class IV to Class VI whitewater and a number of tiring portages. 30 miles might not seem so long, but it is. Although a few people have done the entire stretch in a day, most parties take two or three days and come out the bottom feeling pretty beat up.

So imagine that you've put on and spent your two or so wonderful and challenging days making your way downstream. After you've paddled most of the canyon, exhilarated by the beauty and great whitewater and exhausted by the portages, you come to a rapid that has all the earmarks of Certain Death. The river rounds a sharp corner and goes through a rock sieve, then immediately over a 20 foot waterfall mostly onto a pile of rocks. Although at certain levels one side of the second falls can be run if you put in below the sieve, together these drops form a rapid about as ugly as you can imagine and everything that I've ever learned about running difficult rapids safely says, "you will be hurt or killed if you mess with this." At a minimum you would rate the danger *very* high. I'm fairly certain that everybody who has ever scouted that drop has thought that a mistake above the sieve would be fatal. If you weren't trapped and drowned by the sieve, surely the falls would mangle and kill you.

However, one fine day a number of years ago a paddler missed the eddy in front of the sieve and swam. His friends watched from upstream as he disappeared into the frothing rocks, and with hearts sinking, were certain he was dead. But despite all odds and all our collective wisdom, instead his boat wedged in the boulders underwater and he was stripped out of it, swam through the sieve and over the falls, through the horrendously violent water smashing on sharp granite boulders, and received not a scratch, not the slightest bruise. After scrambling through the huge talus blocks around the portage as fast as they could, his friends found him below the falls, laying there calmly on a midstream boulder and peering into the water for his kayak. It came out the bottom, more or less – the end completely shredded as though a grenade had exploded inside the bow. Those of you who have ever tried to saw through a polyethylene kayak will realize that his boat was dealing with forces of a different order. Yet, the paddler was unscathed and lived to paddle many another day.

What is the moral of the story? Whenever I hear assertions that some rapid is "unrunnable" or that a mistake is "Certain Death" – or even catch myself saying such things – I think back to that incident as a reminder that we may know much less about rivers than we think, and much less about the limits of the sport than we imagine. The rub of the matter is that the world doesn't have to conform to our desires or our assertions of what will happen. Danger is not fixed. Certain Death may not be certain at all.

And yet, after this completely amazing episode, there was a second, much sadder situation at this same rapid not long ago. A group of seven paddlers came down, didn't realize where they were, and flushed into the sieve. One died, two were trapped in caves and had to be rescued or would have drowned, and three others were seriously injured with broken bones. One was unscathed but scared shitless, having had a clear look at the nearest miss he will ever be likely to experience. Certain Death was certain that time.

None of this should surprise us; after all, it is the nature of our sport to push and challenge and question the things that others assert are limits. But you know, even as I say that, I think back to that single critical question I mentioned above, the single thing we would like to know, but never will: "will I die if I mess up and have to swim that rapid?" In the end, maybe the only thing that is certain is that we will always question. After 25 years paddling Class V, I can agree that there are many things I don't know about rivers, but as far as that one question and that one rapid go, I've seen enough and I know my answer.

***

Making Sense of Death

A number of years ago more than ten excellent paddlers died within a season, stunning many in the sport and putting a damper on the enthusiasm for pushing hard whitewater. The names included people at the top of the sport like Chuck Kern, Rich Weiss, Doug Gordon, and others who were less well known but extremely experienced, including Dugal Bremner, Tim Gavin, John Foss, Conrad Fourney, and Joel Hathhorne.

Here at the end of the 2007 season, we've had another shock, as three excellent paddlers died in less than a month: Americans Conrad Fourney and Max Lentz, and German Tim Weinmann, each in a situation that can only be considered bizarre. None of the cases had a clear cause, and all of them lead to a sinking feeling about the sport. More than once after the loss of a friend, I have asked myself whether it is worth it.

Despite all the publicity, the fact is there are not very many deaths in kayaking. Unfortunately, each year there seems to be another name to add, like that of Brennan Guth, a superb young paddler and friend of mine who drowned several years ago in a bizarre and heart-rending accident. Equally unfortunately, a great many of the deaths on rivers can be summed up as freak accidents or bizarre happenings. Those of us who feel the loss of friends try to gain some insight from their passing.

The desire to find a clear cause for death is powerful. Finding a reason gives us a salve for the wound, and the desire goes far beyond anything rational. It makes the death easier to handle, but also, knowing that cause, we can now hold it as a talisman to ward away the same thing from happening to us. I am as guilty of that as anybody. I feel the loss of my friends acutely and have spent many, many long nights staring into the darkness. I pour over accident reports and talk to people who seek resolution, but I have long realized there are many questions that will never be answered. The river never gives all the answers, and the hurt remains alive even after decades have passed.

The problem is, there are an infinite number of bizarre things that can happen on a river. Some things are more common, while others only ever happen once.

In that difficult season ten years ago, *Paddler* magazine ran a number of articles on the theme of the accidents and the problem of "raising the ante", and asked to reprint one of my essays, "Why I paddle class V." There was a push to reevaluate the river rating scale, and to incorporate more safety training.

My German friends were deeply sympathetic to the problem. After a rash of members died in pins, broaches, entrapments in the 1980s, the German elite kayaking group AKC, the "Alpiner Kayak Club" instituted a serious program of safety training, developing most of the techniques that are standard today. However, despite knowing a great deal more and people generally being more highly trained, the deaths still happen.

In many cases, the accidents largely look like an issue of being in the wrong spot at the wrong time. This is a truly unsatisfying answer because it hides the fact we can't tell head of time where the wrong spot might be. Most of the spots were only identifiable after something completely unexpected and desperate happened. In a number of cases, some of the very same lines had been paddled by another member of the group literally a few seconds before without any problem. It is the seeming arbitrariness of this that is so difficult to make peace with.

A brief history makes this apparent.

In the late 1990s, Rich Weiss was the best slalom racer in the US and one of the top two or three in the world. He was a phenomenally skilled paddler and river runner. He died when he did not clear a waterfall, became trapped in a small "room of doom" pocket and his partner was unable to reach him to help. To underscore the tragedy to the point of being unbearable, Rich's pregnant wife was waiting downstream at the take out.

Rich died running a rapid well within his abilities. In fact, he'd run it the day before, and although class V, it was probably two grades easier than he could do technically. To those who knew him it was inconceivable he would have had any problem with that drop. That theme runs through many of the deaths. Some though, are even stranger.

Max Lentz, an excellent young paddler from Missoula, died on a class IV rapid on the upper Gauley last fall. He and others of his group had been running creeky lines for several days, when Max drowned after his boat somehow got caught in a crack deep underwater. He and multiple members of his group had run that same line several times in the preceding days, and two other paddlers had run the same line just seconds before him. Somehow, as he came through, he became trapped in a crack that was completely underwater. Another paddler was right behind him and the very competent group immediately tried to extricate him, but all attempts failed. The question that was impossible to answer was, how did his boat get wedged in the crack in the first place? As best anybody could tell, the water level apparently suddenly decreased right as he went through the critical spot, allowing his boat to wedge down, then surged back to submerge Max completely underwater.

There probably is some reasonable physical explanation, but this was truly an "act of God." How does such a strange thing get incorporated into our knowledge? Nobody could ever scout and paddle a line with this kind of assumption. The fact is, you can be an excellent paddler and yet die in what looks like a simple rapid for reasons you cannot see and cannot know.

Conrad Fourney, a veteran of the Stikine and tremendously experienced paddler, died in Nutcracker on the NF Payette in August, shocking the Idaho paddling community. It was a class V rapid on a well-known, difficult river, but also a rapid he'd run hundreds of times. Members of his group think he went through the hole to the left of the Nut and his sprayskirt blew. Whatever the reason, his water-filled boat broached against a fan rock just downstream and he was able to get out, but the current washed him into an underwater obstruction close to the left bank and flagged him around it. Conrad had an air pocket over his head from the fast current, could move and gesture for several minutes, but numerous attempts to rescue him failed and he drowned.

Tim Weinmann, one of Germany's finest young paddlers, died on the Heiligenkreuz gorge of the Venter Ache last October. While showing several paddlers down the run, he was hammered in a rapid he had run dozens of times before, and swam. He signaled his companions, waving and pointing downstream, which they took to mean he was fine and would swim after his boat. He had at least 100 meters to the next whitewater. When they looked at him again, he was face down washing into the next rapid. There was a 24 hour search for the body, which was found in an eddy downstream. He was 26 years old and in tremendous physical condition. The bizarre possibility of a heart attack pends the outcome of an autopsy.

Strange problems are not the exception. They are the rule. The list of past deaths is filled with such stories.

Chuck Kern was one of the best river runners in the history of the sport, and died on a fairly simple move on the Black Canyon of the Gunnison. Chuck attempted what appeared to be a boof, but which was actually a thin shelf bridging a sieve. Instead of skipping over the boof, his bow dropped into the sieve. All attempts to reach him failed and his body was not retrieved until the dam upstream was turned off several days later. Dugal Bremner died in a crack exposed on a class IV rapid at lower water on the Silver fork of the American River. The team scouted the rapid, which was a longish slide. The main features looked like crossing waves, but actually were formed by a bedrock crack running in the direction of the current; the boat settled into this siphon. He was stable for some time, but unable to get his boat to release. Two other members waded to his boat and got ahold of it, but were actually sucked into and through the siphon, popping up downstream. Finally, both Dugal and his boat were wedged underwater and he drowned. Brennan Guth swam out of a drop on the Rio Palquin in Chile, a rapid much easier than the extremely difficult rapids he'd just been running in the hours before. The swim washed Brennan into a cave, where he held himself spread eagled across the sides against the current for more than an hour until he succumbed to exhaustion and was swept underwater. His partner, an equally experienced paddler and a long time safety instructor - who to my knowledge and experience has always been one of the most safety conscious paddlers in existence and *never* without adequate safety gear - didn't have a throw rope this one time.

Joel Hathhorne missed a small eddy at the top of a cascade on the first descent of Warren Creek, probably due to the same kind of misreading as Chuck. His body was never found. John Foss literally disappeared right in the middle of a Class IV+ rapid on a first descent in Peru, to the stunned bewilderment of his partners who had run the same line 30 seconds before. His body was found two weeks later far downstream. Pablo was stuffed under and pinned by a log in a chute, invisible in the backwash of a hole. The first paddler of his group had plunged into the hole, bounced off the log, and immediately eddied out to warn the others. Before he could, Pablo was already in the middle of the rapid, hit the hole and went under the log. Within a few seconds his hand groped above the surface and his partners desperately did everything they could, jumping in, grabbing it, hitting it with a throw rope, trying to shinny out on the log – all to no avail. Tim Gavin, who probably knew the Upper Blackwater River better than anybody else, died there getting sucked into an undercut on a rapid he'd named years before, gruesomely and ironically, "Just a matter of time".

And there are the dozens or even hundreds of times other people have come ever so close to being in the above group. I'm one of them. Among other things, I've been pinned several times underwater in desperate situations, each one of them completely bizarre. One of them involved being wedged between the bottom and a submerged log in what appeared to be a simple, straightforward rapid. It was a silent, desperate struggle underwater, and then a swim downstream and a pummeling on some rocks before I reached safety. After retrieving my boat and returning to the rapid to figure out what happened, it took several minutes of careful and very puzzled looking before I saw the log, buried deep underwater in a wave and essentially invisible. It was just another drop out of dozens of class IV drops on a class V run, as well as being at least two grades easier than several other drops I'd already run, and a drop nobody ever would have scouted. Even if they had, they couldn't have seen the fatal hazard lurking there. To add to all these, I've rescued other paddlers who found themselves in unpredictable and nearly fatal situations. I've been told by friends, or heard through the grapevine, about dozens of other situations where the person was stuffed through a cave, a sieve or siphon, trapped under a log, hung up on rebar sticking out of a submerged cement block, tangled with underwater debris, and popped out somewhere downstream safely.

These more striking situations grade into the mishaps that virtually every paddler has, things that end up being personal fears, or even the punch line to a local joke. However, the horror stories capture the imagination, particularly when you're among the ghosts who can relate. All of them underscore the complexity of what may happen, as well as the limits of what we really know out there. We can be extraordinarily experienced and skilled, take care of everything we see, and still not take care of the one unseen key that determines whether we live or die.

A few general lessons:

Lesson 1: Virtually no deaths happen on cutting edge whitewater. Essentially all of them occurred on rapids that were well within the abilities of the kayakers.

Lesson 2: While we believe we have an acceptable level of control on the river, in virtually every case there was something additional that occurred which the paddler couldn't have prepared for.

Lesson 3: You can die in a simple rapid. The flip side of this is, you also can get away with the most astonishing misjudgements and errors. There is no accounting for this, but a prudent person would choose good judgment and fewer errors as the way to go.

Lesson 4: Error cascades: When one thing goes wrong, it often leads to another and another in what I call an error cascade. The water magnifies each error and carries it into the future in a powerful way. The key in kayaking is to stay in control, and when that isn't completely possible, to quickly bring any mistake back into control. In a sense, a major part of kayaking includes the skills of constant and creative correction to keep from falling into an error cascade with a bad ending. You should assume that any error cascade may have a bad ending.

Lesson 5: Very infrequently, in the wrong spot, even one simple decision can lead to an error that is not retrievable. Most unfortunately, those are almost always spots that you can-not see ahead of time: a thumb-sized stick that catches your life jacket, an underwater obstruction, a rock with a crack just wide enough for your paddle blade if it comes in at just a particular angle, or another that just fits your foot if you happen to be swimming and kick at that particular instant at a certain water level. Accidents are always somewhere in the details.

Lesson 6: no matter how well conditioned you are, your body may fail you. There are limits to what it can do or survive. Extreme alpinist and tough guy Marc Twight got a lot of mileage out of saying he trained like a maniac in order to make it harder for mountains to kill him. Well, that was Marc's acumen for publicity more than an accurate reflection of reality, as I'm sure he knows. Mountains and rivers are not out to kill us, and they most certainly are not adversaries. They are beautiful physical wonders completely unconcerned about our existence. If we are going to live with them for a while – whether that is a few min-utes, days or weeks – mountains and rivers simply have certain hazards that we must learn to deal with, physically and mentally. Our skill at adventure sports proves it's possible to do that to an amazing and inspiring degree, but only when we are prepared and in excellent condition.

Lesson 7: It is our own decision to be in those places, so it is likewise our responsibility to have the skills and con-ditioning to do it as safely as we can. Our adventure sports are challenging precisely because those environments are only partially predictable. The unpredictability is a major element of what draws us there; so learn your skills well and always be open to learning more. Rivers have been practicing what they do a lot longer than any of us have been kayaking. Perhaps the greatest lesson they can teach is that we should never stop learning.

Lesson 8: If you are worried about getting injured or dying while kayaking, that is a useful concern that should be channeled into positive action. Get better conditioned, work on your roll as well as all your other paddling and rescue skills. A paddler can narrow the range of problems by a healthy safe attitude, having good gear and partners, choosing runs carefully. If worry or fear cripples your fun, then seek solutions. If that doesn't work, back off or find another sport.

Lesson 9: The numbers don't lie – overall, kayaking is a safe sport. You can paddle and enjoy rivers safely for decades. But it is equally true that a single ugly experience can weigh heavily on our enjoyment and attitude, and in extremely unfortunate situations - just like in having a drunk driver hit you or tripping and falling down the stairs at home – it is possible to get injured or killed. Nobody has a sure and certain path. And revealingly, those who do have sure and certain paths often eagerly give them up to find something more interesting.

The beauty of rivers is in large part the same kind of beauty that good music has. It has patterns that delight us and evoke our deepest feelings of excitement, awe, and mystery. Even the simplest surf wave is changing and surging, and even the simplest eddyline is a wonder of complexity. Add up a river full of such things and you have the treasures of the planet spread before you. The river is the essence of creativity and change, creating rapids and features of boundless variety. But among those changes and slight unpredictabilities – the very things that create our pleasure – lie features that can injure and kill us.

The river doesn't care. It is a force of nature, following the laws of physics and showing us continually that flowing water contains all the beauty and magic of the world. Learning to engage that magic is what creates our sport. Challenge and fun, as well as danger and death, all come from the same place. It is up to you to decide what that means – and to treat it with the care and respect it deserves.

***

Fear in Kayaking – Part 1

For lack of better judgment, I've taken on the topic of fear in kayaking, which is a huge area that no single essay will exhaust. Even the three parts of this essay are really only a first exploration. The overall hope is that readers will develop their own views and questions so there can be a community airing of ideas.

Over the years I've written only a handful of stories or comments about fearful situations because so little of my own experience in kayaking has been fearful. I paddle for overwhelmingly positive experiences, so fear has not been a driving force or a common occurrence. However, I've been asked questions about fear hundreds of times by all sorts of people, so I'm well aware that it is a frequent and serious part of many people's paddling. I also have had some personal experiences with it, as well as situations where usually it would appear – getting badly worked by the river, having several serious accidents, rescues, and a number of friends who have died.

In laying out the science of what's known about fear, I am only describing enough to serve a practical purpose. A lot is known about fear in terms of its physiological events and the neural pathways involved. If you want to follow this technical information up, go to the library or get online and you'll google up more than you can ever read. My reason for avoiding most of this is that it will not help in any practical way. For instance, knowing that the amygdala is an integral part of the fear pathway is not going to help you run a rapid, or deal with emotional debris from a past frightening situation. For that reason nearly all the discussion will be experiential because that is where we live, feel, think, and learn.

Introduction

Fun and fear in kayaking often appear side by side for many people. While most of us remember our river experiences as fun and satisfying, others have had an uphill battle from the beginning, fighting doubts and fear but knowing the sport held much more for them. Understanding the interplay of all these feelings requires knowing a lot about the physiology, psychology, and experience of kayaking. As a start, consider a classic beginner's story. Probably every reader has been told of something like this or even experienced it themselves.

A young friend of mine named Steve recently asked me to teach him how to kayak. Steve had wanted to kayak whitewater for as long as he could remember because it looked like the coolest and funnest sport ever. The problem was, several years ago he'd tried kayaking for the first time and gotten badly scared. An acquainttance of his who had been paddling for four or five years took him down a class III river at high water without any preparation or practice. "He said I'd be fine, gave me some gear, and down we went."

Steve did fine for the first quarter mile. "The river was great! The sun was shining and I felt like I was riding a rollercoaster on top of the world." Then they hit the first rapid. "The waves were huge! Well, I know they weren't that big, but they looked like they were way over my head. I lost my balance on the first one and fell over. I didn't know what to do and suddenly I was upsidedown and out of air and I just lost it. I felt the boulders going past my head and it freaked me out. I let go of the paddle and started tearing at the spray skirt and it wouldn't come off. For a few seconds I thought I wouldn't be able to get out, and that freaked me even more, until I finally ripped the spray skirt off and tore myself out of the boat."

He was coughing, his nose was full of water, and he swam to shore while his friend chased the boat. "I got really cold and was shivering, but I wanted to keep trying." They set off again, and the same scenario repeated itself. "I felt good, but every time I got paddling I'd flip in a rapid. I started dreading the next rapid. I wanted to run them so bad, but I just couldn't. I didn't know what to do. My balance was shot. I totally lost all my confidence."

He swam every rapid for the rest of the day and it was a terrible experience. "My friend tried to show me how to roll, but I just couldn't get it. Nothing worked. I felt defeated and bummed out."

Now, three years later, he was ready to try again. "I hate going to the river and feeling scared. I know if I just learn it right I can do it. But when I stand there and think about getting in a kayak, my hands start shaking. I'm really scared, and I just hate that."

As my friend's story shows, fear is an easy thing to experience on a river. While some people can bootstrap themselves up with little or no instruction, most can't and every one of us can multiply stories about friends like Steve. I sometimes wonder how many people are out there who would love to be kayakers, but couldn't get over that initial bad experience, or some other fearful situation that came along when they were learning. Running whitewater is one of the most exciting, beautiful and fun things you can experience, and being able to use a kayak is like having your own private magic carpet. But fear ruins enthusiasm and will ground even the best magic carpet. As we will discuss below, in many ways it is also the twin brother of excitement, and whether the experience moves toward one or the other depends on many things, including your basic physiology, your prior learning, what you expect, and what you have practiced. Fear is something that many kayakers have to face at some point, but yet it also is something that many experienced kayakers don't talk about at all, leaving newcomers to work their way through what can easily become a psychological minefield.

You might think it is a paradox, but the same things that make whitewater kayaking so incredibly fun, also gear it perfectly to tweak many simple and powerful fears. Having the control to glide across and engage the river's power is thrilling and deeply satisfying. Being at its mercy is just the opposite. This yin and yang exchange is the underlying dynamic that makes kayaking the greatest sport in the world.

Just think about Steve's story and make a list of the things that are potentially fear-provoking for a first time kayaker. There is the fear from lack of control mentioned above – the kayak is hard to balance and seems on the verge of tipping over half the time. Even steering the boat is frustrating because it wants to turn with a mind of its own. Then there is the fear of being trapped inside the kayak, unable to get out, or of being upsidedown in the water and not being able to breathe. If the person goes out in moving water, suddenly everything changes again and all the budding control skills from flat water are red-lined. Once the person heads downstream, balance is even harder, and there's the fear of being swept away into some un-known disaster by forces he or she can't control. And to top it off, when the person tries to get out of the current to take a break, he has to move against it. Suddenly the water's power comes alive and prevents him from getting to safety. If you listen carefully to people describing how that feels, you'll even hear the sense of being threatened by a living beast that wouldn't let them go.

If you're not careful, or maybe if you're just unlucky, all those things can be experienced within the first few minutes by a beginner in class I and II whitewater – and lead to them never coming back. The bottom line for a kayaker is, even in simple situations, having trouble out on a river readily evokes a sense of helplessness, vulnerability, and lack of control that are the very heartbeat of fear.

Fear is a totally normal and good thing. It's an essential survival mechanism, and without it humans wouldn't be around. As a working definition, we can consider it a general emotional state that we experience when threatened by present or im-pending danger. Its purpose is to improve our survival by avoid-ing the danger, running away, or super-charging us to aggres-sively defend ourselves.

The problem we face as kayakers is that a fear reaction gets in the way of activities we want to try. Our evolved sense of survival crashes head-on into our choice of 21st century recreation. Even if there isn't any disaster looming, that ancient question of *"are you sure you should be doing this?"* can echo through our minds and interfere with what we need to learn to have fun at our chosen sport.

People don't have this reaction to a sport like baseball or volleyball. The difference lies in the kind of game being played. Most sports are set up for competition with other humans. Humans put the ball in play, control the pace, and there are lots of rules for what kinds of movements you can do and when you can do them. To play at all, you have to learn a rulebook that some committee wrote up. But in adventure sports, of which whitewater kayaking is probably one of the most demanding, you are playing a game with nature. There are no rules in that game except the laws of physics, and the psychology that governs your ability to learn and react. Despite your gear being space-aged plastic and fiber composites, you are playing with very elemental forces. There's no rule committee and no referee - only God and Nature. You are interacting with the forces that made this planet and you are trying to survive and have fun. So the bottom line isn't a flyball caught by the second baseman to end the inning, or telling everybody to wait because you sprained your ankle catching a frisbee. It's primal stuff, like being able to roll your kayak upright so you can breathe. Or like touching the powerful chaotic heart of the river and moving with it in perfect synchrony. The river flows powerfully whether you are ready or not. It never makes allowances for you. It doesn't care if you are struggling or hurt. In it, at every second you are dealing with the real shit, which is exactly what makes it so damn much fun.

Thus, the critical difference is that kayaking and all other adventure sports are games with real consequences. The fun of paddling comes through the balance between the skills you develop and the threat of painful mistakes. The river is totally fair and plays no favorites. This creates a powerful enticement to learn - the joy of control that has potential punishment lurking in the background.

The first time you run a rapid brings all these elemental things to a boil. It will be the funnest, wildest ride you ever had, the ragged water rushing you along, the bank so far away, and you ride enmeshed in a world of movement and power in the living water. No amusement park ride can ever be as intense as that experience. The first time you surf a wave brings it all out again. The sense of rising up and sliding down the face of a living wave, of carving into it back and forth, feeling it slip by beneath you. It's been over 25 years since I first did that, and I still get goosebumps because I can remember it so vividly. And that is just the beginning in Class II water.

While joy is the positive side coming from the challenge of skill and control, fear is the negative side. It is the threat of consequences from the river, either from your mistakes in skill or judgment, or simply from events out of your control. It may also be from completely illogical and unrealistic worries.

As your skills develop, you seek out places where the difficulty fits your ability to control, or tests that ability. Somewhere in the full range of Class I to class VI+, from creeks to big water, you'll find an infinite number of such challenges. If you love the water, it contains more challenges than you can face in a life-time. Throughout these, the river will always remind you that this is the real world, and you will find not only the challenges that you see and come upon knowingly, but others that come suddenly and from unexpected directions. When that happens you can readily tip from the most positive feelings into the negative.

Although you should remember that kayaking is actually a very safe sport, in the longer term you can bank on having a few obnoxious experiences. It goes with the territory. You may flip and get caught on an eddyline, and suddenly the eskimo roll you did 100 times in a row and were so proud of in the pool doesn't work as you're spun down the no-man's-land between the current and the eddy, running out of air, suddenly feeling at the mercy of the water. In an instant, out of the huge fun rises a feeling that you cannot put chains on or control. If you are finally able to roll in the runout, you may feel empowered or maybe just thankful you hung in there. If you have to punch out of your boat and go for a swim, choking on water and smacking your shins on the rocks is likely going to be painful and frightening. The level of control you feel and your attitude toward it make all the difference. Being out of control and not being able to breathe is guaranteed to evoke fear, and that fear will be learned and affect your decisions and feelings toward rivers and kayaking.

So let's delve into the physiology of fear in more detail. The processes are primitive and powerful. Primitive in the sense that they bypass the areas of the brain used in rational thinking and instead, follow pathways in the nervous system that go directly to the centers that control emotion. It's like having a fuse that goes directly to a bomb. A fear response can be learned in an instant and last your entire lifetime.

Physiology of fear

Consider the nuts and bolts of what happens inside your body when you get frightened. The first and simplest fear reaction is something you've probably read about in a psychology class, and is termed the "fight or flight" survival response. Probably all of you have experienced it. It has been extensively studied, mapped out most recently using fMRI imaging techniques of which parts of the brain are active when people are experiencing fear. Physiologically, it's a complex set of automatic survival responses that are completely outside of your conscious control, and which get you ready for major physical action, like protecting yourself by fighting the grizzly bear that's attacking you, or running like a jackrabbit from a pack of ferocious weasels.

Consider this situation:

One sunny summer day I was with my children at a popular swimming spot on the Blackfoot river, when I heard a bunch of yells. A 6-year old boy had been wading out at the end of an underwater gravel bar far out into the river. It crumbled underneath him, and he had been swept away by the current. He

128

couldn't swim and was frantically trashing and choking badly. The young father went into full fight or flight mode, with adrenaline pumping, jumped in after his son and managed to grab ahold. But he couldn't swim either, so they were both choking and sinking as they were sucked under on the eddyline and pulled downstream. An entire beach full of people stood there and watched, none of them moved. I dove in, swam up the eddyline, judged where to break out and came up behind. I put the father in a headlock and propped him up, talking right into his ear quietly and firmly the whole time. "Everything's fine, just hold your son's head above the water. I'll get you to shore. Don't fight me, relax and let yourself float." I let us float down past the troublesome eddyline, got them to shore, and the mother sat there holding her son, sobbing, while he crumbled into her arms. The father was still coughing heavily and so exhausted he couldn't sit up, laying there flat on his back with his eyes closed and could only whisper "thanks."

And so let's think about fear. The kid and the parents did not know enough about rivers to understand what might happen, so their ignorance of real consequences created a dangerous situation. A little fear would have been a good thing if it had led to a sense of caution about wading out too far. Once something happened, they didn't have the skills to handle it, and their reactions were driven by that Neanderthal survival instinct, which is completely ineffective or worse in a river because water doesn't act the way a saber toothed tiger does. Getting all pumped up with adrenaline and jabbing the tiger with a spear or beating him over the head with a rock might be fine, but jumping into a river and flailing only gets you in deep trouble.

The feeling of helplessness the mother had is one of the most frightening things possible, and one I can vouch for as terrifying. A nightmare I had several times when my children were small, was having one of them fall into a swollen muddy river. I remember the feeling of despair – they've disappeared, the water is murky and I can't see them or even find them to save them. Despite all my skills and understanding of the water, all my national level swimming and Class V kayaking, I'm helpless as they die. Their innocence and vulnerability, coupled with my knowledge of what could happen, was a horrible mix. That was a dream I could have done without.

So what happened to the father? The fuse gets lit when you perceive a threat. That perception can be sudden and very simple. For the father, it was seeing his son disappear into the water. For a beginning kayaker it might be flipping upsidedown before he or she is able to roll and suddenly groping for air. There is a rush of sensations and threats - the sense of being trapped in the boat, not knowing what to do, water shoved up your nose and half choking, needing to breath and not being able to. The first step leads to the "fight or flight" reaction.

There are two primary fear reactions. Most direct and immediate is a pathway that entirely bypasses your thinking process, literally going from whatever senses lit the fuse, right to a small region of the brain called the amygdala, which is the brain center that controls emotionality. It is sometimes called the "eye to amygdala" pathway, or the "low road." The other route has more input and takes a little longer because it goes through your sensory cortex before it reaches the deeper brain centers. However, both routes go to the amygdala and start the fireworks.

The response from the amygdala is a surge of reactions that lead from it to another part of the brain called the hypothalamus, which controls the fight or flight response. The hypothalamus activates two parallel pathways which reinforce each other. One is the sympathetic branch of the autonomic nervous system which acts through nerve pathways and the bloodstream, and the other is the adrenal-cortical system which acts only through the bloodstream. It's a little like lighting a stick of dynamite from both ends. Both converge to give a double rev-up of your body from every angle provided by blood chemistry and the nervous system. For the fight response, think of transforming into the Hulk, for the flight response, think of a terrified jackrabbit.

When the sympathetic nervous system is activated, the physiological processes that aid in fight or flight speed up, while those that don't are shut down. These are controlled by the nerve impulses go to the glands and smooth muscles, and those that go to the adrenal medulla, a brain region that releases stress hormones into the bloodstream, the best known being adrenaline. These stress hormones have a set of effects that cascade through your nervous and muscular systems.

Meanwhile the hypothalamus also activates the adrenal-cortical system. It does this by releasing something called CRF (corticotropin-releasing factor) into the pituitary gland, which is a central controller of hormones in the body, and a major center of the endocrine system. The pituitary in turn releases ACTH (adreno-corticotropic hormone) which reaches the adrenal cortex, where it in turn activates the release of a literal pharmacopeia of several dozen other hormones.

Almost instantaneously, this torrent of adrenaline and dozens of other hormones cause massive changes. The whole thing can ramp up in only a second or two: activating your nervous, blood, respiratory, and muscular systems. It yields a drastically increased heart rate and blood pressure (a pounding heart), dilated pupils, the hairs on your skin sticking up, veins constricted to shunt blood to the active muscles, a flood of glucose into the blood-stream from the liver, tensed muscles, dilation of the airways, sweating (think sweaty palms), digestion is shut down (causing butterflies and even nausea). The reinforced response through the two major pathways serves to "double up" the effects throughout the entire body.

This is serious business. It's the biggest explosion of the wildest chemicals your body can produce, and not something you brush away or easily control after it's started. It's a whole-body reaction that bypasses rationality to prime you for heavy-duty action. The emotions you are aware of may be anxiety, fear, alarm, but your conscious thought comes AFTER the chemical fireworks have lit up every switchboard you have.

From our evolutionary history, each of the above changes has a survival value, such as increased oxygen flow from dilation of your airways. The increases in oxygen and glucose in your blood heighten the responsiveness of your muscles, and maximize the force they can generate. Some additional responses that you can observe in others and yourself are changes in facial expression (tense facial and jaw muscles), higher tone of voice, increased talkativeness, stiffer posture. In extreme cases, people can freeze, even start crying, losing control of their bladder and bowels, or collapse into a trembling heap. Normally in our sport, we're dealing with mild degrees of fear where we can still function, but you should keep in mind the continuum of possibilities. I've seen most of them, and if you are around enough different people in enough circumstances, you will too.

However, there are two immediate and extremely important cognitive effects for us kayakers. First, in addition to all the internal fireworks, our attention and ability to think narrow drastically. It's called tunnel vision, and it makes it hard to keep complications or extra details in mind, as you will know if you've ever been really anxious. Remember, it is an unconscious effect due to the massive change in body chemistry and the nervous system's response. This is the point at which the shit has hit the fan, and now we have to respond. But people get tunnel visioned, befuddled, or freeze, unable to make decisions. Second, the emotion comes before rational thought, so these powerful feelings hijack your thinking and drive it. In some situations, people can experience extreme clear-headedness, but this is pretty rare.

These responses can do some incredible things. You've probably heard of the stories of grandmothers lifting cars off of somebody in a wreck. Well, my friend Bob McDougall experienced this himself when a close friend of his was slammed underneath a 1200 pound steel plate that slipped off the lift gate of a truck. It missed Bob by inches, crushed the other guy into the ground, but Bob lifted the damn thing right off his friend. The friend suffered a huge number of broken bones, but lived and is currently doing some serious rehabbing. Bob's a strong guy, but 1200 pounds? That's exactly what he did. Score one for his fight response.

This whole system probably evolved very early in the scheme of animal life, and is shared with essentially all mammals. Other animals such as reptiles and birds also show similar kinds of responses, although their nervous systems are simpler. So from an evolutionary standpoint, this is an "all hands on deck" response from a time when all emergencies were physical. This brings us to the central problem posed for river travelers.

The problem is that we are 21st Century kayakers moving down a whitewater river, and for us now, the critical issue is keeping our heads, preferably never getting fearful, but certainly able to deal with it if suddenly all this heavy-duty chemistry begins pumping through us. This is what sets kayaking apart from many other sports, even other adventure sports, and makes preventing, understanding, and handling the effects of fear so important. There is no other sport or activity where it is so essential to maintain your ability to think and respond appropriately when all hell is breaking loose and your body wants to make you act like a Neanderthal on crack.

Again, the critical problem is that what leads to effective reactions and survival in a river is very different from what works on land. Most, if not all of the primitive responses that were evolved for survival in land scenarios will get you in deeper trouble or killed on a river. Just think of the story above about the guy and his son.

The fight or flight response evolved for a small two-legged primate cruising around on the savannah where there were a lot of big predators. The forms of reaction it is geared to produce – aggressive defense, running away, or freezing – will not work on a river. Instead, your responses have to be controlled through the specialized skills and judgments you've learned for moving water, which is what makes kayaking so difficult. These skills mean the difference between quickly and effortlessly getting out of a predicament or doing something that ruins your day. In the worst of situations, it may even mean life and death.

All these skills, including judgment, must follow a fundamental concept that is expressed well in the martial arts: move with the force, harmonize, and direct it to your own ends. The bottom line is, when you're having trouble in a kayak, you can't fight the river or run from it. You must always be the river's respectful partner in flow – even when it is pummeling you. The shift away from your built-in responses to an intricate set of learned skills, leads us to the *psychology* of fear in kayaking.

***

Fear In Kayaking - Part II:
The Psychology of Fear

The first part of this article dealt with the nuts-and-bolts physiology of fear. It stressed that fear was a hard wired survival mechanism, and that the biggest problem for us as kayakers was that our usual "fight or flight" survival reflexes are strongly evoked in many situations. However, they evolved to have us flee, fight, or freeze to defend ourselves against living predators - responses that are totally inappropriate on a river and actually undermine our safety there. The physics of flowing water determine how effective any response will be, and water is a force of nature – not a living creature that can be bluffed, driven away, or killed. This means our instinctual responses must be avoided, and the reactions channeled into a new set of carefully developed skills that keep us safe in the face of these different threats.

So this second part discusses the *psychology* of fear, which includes the dynamics of when fear is experienced and how we learn it. We will look at how easily fear is learned, and how it can occur in situations where there is no objective danger at all, which leads us to consider the distinction between realistic and unrealistic fears. We will look at the fact fear is just another form of general arousal, a half step away from excitement and fun. The context and the meaning the situation has for you are what separate fear from excitement.

The third part of this series (below) focuses on how we can deal with fear. The primary strategy is to be proactive by carefully developing the physical and mental skills that allow us to understand the river and control our path down it. From these come confidence, the internal tool that keeps us from lighting up the chemical fireworks of fear in the first place. Things are much more complicated when we must react to fear, but for those whose fireworks have already been lit, we can learn skills that help with the difficult task of controlling the reactions. For these reasons, the psychology of learning goes hand in hand with understanding fear in kayaking.

Before we dive into all this, I want to stress one thing. With all the focus being on fear, readers should not overlook an important reality: fear is a derivative reaction that happens when things go wrong, or when we worry they might. However, the reason we're even on the river in a kayak in the first place is that it is the funnest, wildest, greatest sport in the world. The river is a powerful and dynamic environment, and when we learn the skills to handle it, we're set free in a new world, exploring with a magic carpet or our own private space ship. It is as if you took the best amusement park in the world, joined it with the most beautiful surroundings, and then got on intimate terms with God about how he runs the whole show. It's exciting and fascinating, humbling and inspiring. In a word, it's a celebration of life.

So the real issue here is to understand this thing called fear that interferes with our ability to move into this brave new world. Understanding is power, and when used correctly it leads to freedom. This article's goal is to help you understand fear and to set you free.

Learning Fear is easy

There are two simple psychological facts that make it difficult to avoid fear. First, fear can stick its head up anywhere. You don't need to be in a dangerous situation to experience it. It can appear even when you are perfectly safe and there is no objective threat at all. Unfortunately, even if a fear is unrealistic, it can be just as debilitating as any realistic one.

The second is that fear is a potent experience that leads to extremely fast learning. In the first part of the article we talked about the fear pathway through the amygdala. This fires up so quickly and its effects spread so fast through the sympathetic nervous system that memory for fear is a full body experience, learned incredibly easily and lasting forever. It's like a form of super learning. You'd love to be able to do that in school, or on your job, or anyplace in kayaking. Imagine how it would work with a freestyle move – one try and you've got your new trick in the bag and you're on to the next one. It would be like Neo in the movie *The Matrix* - suddenly you just "know" kung fu.

Unfortunately, that fearful super learning only works for the bad stuff that interferes with all the things we want to enjoy. The good learning is slow, fitful, and requires constant practice. The bad learning is virtually instantaneous and can last your entire life. It also can overwhelm years of careful good learning.

Let's consider in a little more detail the psychology how and why fear is learned so fast. A fear response is the easiest thing to learn because it is the most important for survival. Our psychology is defined by a time when we weren't the main predator on the planet. We were small, weak, slow two-legged primates in a world full of more powerful and fearsome animals. Our one main advantage was our remarkable ability to learn, and that ability is in full view with fear. In a predator-prey world like that, we could be wrong about a lot of things that didn't matter, but a situation where we could be killed was an absolute. So our remarkable ability served the primary purpose of small prey – to fast-track learning fear, even to the extent that it over-powers everything else, and avoid potentially dangerous situa-tions rather than test them.

As a hair-trigger system, learning fear is geared to err on the side of caution and avoid danger. This works because it is far more effective to have a lot of false alarms than to be critically wrong just once. Think of what this means for a deer – it tends to run first and ask questions later or not at all. Or think of our tribal forebearers – when they heard a peculiarly menacing growl they didn't think, "Hey, that sounded like the pissed off tiger that ate the Smith family last week. I think I'll check it out!" No, they ran like hell instead. From the standpoint of survival, it's better to be wrong and safe than possibly test something uncertain and end up dead. Evolutionarily speaking, there are few things more final than being eliminated from the gene pool.

Now, think of what this means with kayaking. We're 21st Century humans looking to have fun, but with multi-million year-old limbic systems ready to steer us clear of danger. From the very beginning of learning the sport, we are constantly in situations where we are testing our control and understanding, while that limbic system, the bedrock of our nervous system, is ready with its finger on the fear button. The sport itself tends to push us closer to the edge of a system that already has a hair-trigger. With this combination, it's no wonder that so many people end up grappling with some aspect of fear.

Fortunately, there's a wonderful counterbalance to this — which is that for all the time you spend not feeling fear, all that testing and learning of control, you're excited and focused, surfing waves and running rapids, feeling your way intimately into one of the planet's deep powers. These are hugely potent and rewarding experiences that every single one of us knows and loves. They are the opposite image of the fear, and you cannot consider fear with-out thinking about the feelings that lead us to be on the river in the first place. The chemical fireworks of fun, challenge, and excitement are the close brothers of fear, and are constantly enticing us to come along with them. Our job is to follow them without getting waylaid by the Limbic Big Bro.

The physiology we discussed in the first part of the article describes the mechanics of fear, but we aren't mechanical robots, and our emotions aren't just mechanical responses to stimuli. We have intentions, thoughts, will, feelings, memories, and desires. We have passions and senses of humor and we make decisions about all these things. But the difficult thing with the fear reaction is that it literally has a mind of its own that veers strongly away from any-thing we control within us.

Remember, fear occurs at a level underneath your conscious will or control, because the limbic system and pathways through the amygdala and hypothalamus are outside the higher areas of the brain through which you exert conscious control and awareness. This means that once fear starts, it tends to shanghai your control panel, overriding the other things you've learned, shov-ing aside all your fine tuned sensibilities and intentions, and even your ability to control your own arms and legs.

It also means that once fear is learned, it is very powerful and resistant to change. It is diffused throughout your body and stored in ways you can't access consciously, so is difficult to get at using rational thinking. People can spend years in therapy undoing the effect of one serious fearful experience from an accident, mugging, or other trauma. A situation just a few seconds long can be retained for your entire life, so it's not something you want to fool around with if you have any choice in the matter.

All these things together are why whitewater kayaking is probably the hardest adventure sport. The river is always challenging us for control, throwing curveballs, and always has an element of unpredictability. It is the essence of change, and kayaking is built on exploring its changes. Even at its simplest levels for a beginner, the exploration involves testing what seem at first to be dangerous situations with newly minted skills, so it tends to crash into our evolved fear mechanisms.

These different elements are why kayaking is also perhaps the most rewarding and fascinating adventure sport. It requires a wonderful mix of movement skills and great flexibility in using them to the point of pure improvisation. This yin and yang aspect mirror perfectly one of the main differences between fear and fun, terror and delight – that context and your attitude largely determine the emotional outcome of any event. In most situations, what is going on inside of you controls the emotional results.

You can fear anything

We can learn to fear anything because we can potentially feel threatened and vulnerable in almost any situation. In the extreme, we can even bring a sense of vulnerability to any situation – even when it has no threat at all. That's called baggage. Because adventure sports require learning a new set of skills in a new environment, they are well tuned to finding your baggage.

In a sense, every adventure sport is a long term investigation into fun that requires learning to separate the things that don't matter from the things that do. A great deal of the fun comes learning skills to direct your destiny, which means not being distracted by problems that can be predicted or controlled, or by worries that are irrelevant. Kayaking has a great many lessons to teach us about accurately understanding the world. It can show us truths we would never see otherwise.

Realistic versus Unrealistic Fears

So let's start by separating the realistic from the unrealistic fears. From what I've seen, most of the fears kayakers feel are unrealistic – we're fearful even when in reality we are quite safe. In contrast, a realistic fear is one learned from direct experience of an actual injury and the fear accurately represents the reality of what happened. There probably aren't statistics on this, but in my experience the people with such realistic fears seem to be a tiny minority. Nearly every time I've ever talked with people about their fears, the fear is not based on something dangerous that actually happened to them, but on their anxiety about unknown possibilities and their lack of confidence. There are a lot of people who don't seem to have any direct reason to be fearful. Instead their fears are based on anticipations and doubts, and compounded by other factors.

A friend of mine captured this well. Susan has been paddling for more than ten years. She is solid on Class IV and has a lot of experience paddling the standard runs in Colorado. Yet, she is frightened. When asked why, she admits she's never been hurt. She's most scared of hitting her head on a rock when upsidedown, although she's never hit her head, ever. She's also scared of swimming even though she's never been hurt swimming, and was a national level swimmer for 15 years and went to college with a swimming scholarship. She is in great condition, smart, strong and skilled, can do a roll both sides better with her hands than with a paddle. She would seem to be an ideal candidate for having great confidence and little fear.

Why is she fearful? Here's where the other factors come in. Consider that she paddles only seasonally, from late spring through summer. By the end of the summer she feels great, with good control and a bomber roll. But then she doesn't kayak for 8 months. She's a mother, chemist, professional researcher, and musician, so she has plenty to keep her busy far from any water. When she starts thinking about kayaking again the next spring, the rivers are cold and high. The long lay-off plays with her mind and she starts doubting herself. If she could just paddle a few rivers during the off season, her familiar sense of control would return, but the rivers are frozen and there's no place to go. This slight chink in her armor yields worries, and the worries grow because there is no direct action or practice to counter them. She has huge anticipation and her confidence wanes while her worries take front stage.

When spring comes, she'd like to start out slow and ease into the season, but the runoff in the Rocky Mountain West is geared exactly backwards for that. The water is high, cold and the weather unstable. Even the easy runs are much harder. To compound these worries, her husband is a good class V paddler and while he's fairly patient, he doesn't want to ease into the season, so she has difficulty finding partners and usually is mismatched in attitude and skill level. Once she's out and on the water, there's great relief and a growing sense of confidence as the familiarity of the moves and sensations return with the feeling, "Oh yeah, I can do this." But if she's going with her husband, since he accommodated her on an "easy" run, she feels the next trip has to accommodate him better and is probably going to be harder than she'd like, so in the back of her mind she's already tensing up for that. Paddling would be much easier if she didn't have to juggle all these other concerns. However, like most of us, she lives in the real world and her life is filled with such things.

Obviously, the situation isn't optimal for reinstating control and confidence each year, but it reflects the fact that most people don't have their lives set up to develop perfect confidence and skills in kayaking. Very few do, usually only younger people without many responsibilities. Susan's never even had a bad experience doing all this, but it makes her uncomfortable and she ends up second-guessing herself. This interplay of compounding factors makes it difficult to develop and maintain her confidence, and largely unrealistic fears creep in. Between the layoff, loss of familiarity, harder-than-preferred runs, expectations, no partners who really match her in motivation and comfort zone, there's plenty of fodder for doubts and fear.

This last observation is a theme that runs through most fear. The best course of action is to take small steps, increase your familiarity, and systematically improve your skills and control. Knowing you can do something, knowing that your skills are solid and you are prepared, lead to feeling confident. Competence, control, skill and understanding are the antidotes to most fears, particularly the unrealistic ones. Most fears occur because we try to take bigger steps than we should, attempt to do unfamiliar things, and don't systematically improve our skills and control. Consequently, there is no way our confidence will be solid, because the chinks in the armor are there, ready for the river to work on.

While Susan's situation shows how unrealistic fears can creep into the life of a competent paddler, here is a simpler example of an overwhelming, powerful, yet totally unrealistic fear.

Marie is a friend of mine who has been deathly afraid of water all her life. It stemmed from one incident: on a family vacation when she was 4, she fell off a dock at a small lake. As she briefly floated there at the surface, holding her breath, watching and listening to everything that was going on, her mother went completely bonkers, hysterically screaming, "She's drowning! Help, Help, My baby is drowning!!" It took all of 10 seconds for the father to jump in, scoop up his daughter, and get her to safety. She didn't choke. She wasn't even afraid. But the damage was done because she'd watched her mother come unglued, and that screaming and terror has echoed in her ears ever since. Her phobia is a deep-rooted, reflex fear that to this day, thirty years later, is so powerful it pervades every association she has toward water. Needless to say, when I offered a kayaking lesson, she wasn't interested.

Exaggerated, unrealistic fears restrict and dominate our thoughts, preventing us from exploring and finding the truth about the world. They are false in the sense they do not accurately reflect reality, even though they are real feelings. And while Marie's situation was dramatically produced by her mother in a ten second childhood incident, Susan's is a complicated interaction that has developed over ten years. And think again on the earlier example of my friend Steve's experience when he repeatedly swam that first time out in Class III. That was three hours on a river, and the reality is he took multiple swims and only got wet, a little cold, and choked a couple of times. That's pretty benign. Yet, all that potent emotion pouring through his system converted an annoying and uncomfortable experience into something terrifying. The chief cause was feeling out of control and the threat of being swept into the unknown. These are critical themes in the creation of fear. Once the threshold is reached and the fear reaction begins, those potent chemical fireworks feed the very worst of your inaccurate perceptions.

These examples illustrate that much of our fear comes from ignorance, particularly as beginners, because we simply do not know what the water will do and we don't have the skills to deal with it. You fear what you don't know and can't control, and this becomes especially pronounced when you feel catastrophe looms in every direction.

To deal with fear, we have to separate this untrue, self-created feeling of disaster from what the real dangers are, so we aren't controlled by what amount to powerful, personal superstitions jet fueled by our most potent chemistry.

What is a realistic fear?
Here are two examples of realistic fears.

A recent acquaintance named Tom told me about an incident he'd experienced his second year of kayaking. He flipped

143

upside down in a Class III rapid on an easy run, severely hit his head, suffered multiple skull fractures and had a terrifying and painful time getting out of the river. He then struggled through long term rehabilitation. He loves paddling, went back to it with a vengeance, and is doing very well, having paddled widely and honed his skills up to solid Class IV+. Yet, understandably he finds himself wrestling with deep doubts when confronting rapids, with fear creeping into his best experiences and preventing him from enjoying the sport fully.

I have to say that in my nearly 30 years on rivers and all the accident reports I've ever seen, his was a freak injury. Such things are incredibly infrequent and he was very, very unlucky. Yet, the incident happened and his fear reaction is fully realistic. That fear exists at a deep, physiological level. In effect, he has PTSD – post traumatic stress syndrome – a deep classically conditioned fear based on the trauma of the injury and pain he experienced. Unfortunately, it pervades his whole attitude and experience of kayaking. Currently, I'm helping him on ways to deal with it and he's having a good degree of success.

Another realistic fear is a much more specific one of my own. In 1989 Rob Lesser, Bob McDougall and I set out to do the first self-contained descent of the Grand Canyon of the Stikine in northern British Columbia. We scouted the first huge drop, called Entry Falls, and decided on a line that had worked when Rob and McD did the first (helicopter assisted) descent four years before. However, we couldn't see the critical part because it was hidden by a massive boulder that had shifted positions. McD went first and disappeared over the edge. I gave him time and then came down, only to find as I was entering the drop that he was being annihilated in a powerful hole that swept back into undercuts on both sides. To make a long story short, I avoided the hole and ran the whole rapid out of control. Mean-while, McD was pounded beyond belief, then swept underneath a boulder and just barely managed to scratch his way back to the surface. The ordeal continued, as he was trapped against a sheer cliff with nothing but shattered rock above him for 400 vertical feet, and a massive class V rapid in front of him. Being a big wall climber, he headed up the improbable wall and somehow made it. To hear the whole story, you should take a look at my book on the Stikine when it comes out. The effect on him was that he never again did hard Class V, and the effect on me was that I developed an aversion to running things blind, and to assuming a drop is still fine because it was run four years before. In fact, I will never run something hard I haven't scouted. I have younger, highly skilled friends who run hard things seat of the pants regularly, on verbal instructions without looking at the drop themselves. But I will never do that again because that one problem was one too many. I don't know whether to call it a fear, but let's just say I have a deep dislike about not knowing where I'm going on a Class V+ river. That feeling was created entirely by watching my best friend come as close as it's possible to drowning, and being helpless to do anything about it. Importantly, this fear is incorporated in a fully realistic way into my entire approach to rivers.

The above examples from Steve, Susan, Marie, Tom, McD and me could be expanded by thousands of others. They show that you can learn fear from a wide variety of experiences, some of which represent realistic dangers, and others that reflect only a false sense of threat. It also shows they are then incorporated in many ways. Susan continues to kayak and intermittently feel fearful and confident. That near disaster on the Stikine didn't stop me from going up there three more times and loving the place, as well as paddling hundreds of other difficult runs. McD still paddles, but the hard-core expedition fire went out. Interestingly, all these years later he feels good about what happened – he was dealt one of the worst situations you could ever imagine and he handled it. Steve is still working on his paddling skills, warily but with great enthusiasm. Marie probably will never do more than wade ankle deep in a lake, and will not get in a raft or kayak. Tom is a serious paddler working through his underlying fear by gaining control of it and his paddling skills. This range shows our reactions are heavily dependent on the context, and what we interpret as dangerous or threatening, and especially, whether we can develop a sense of control over the threatening aspects.

Arousal – emotional jet fuel

A key element in our reaction is the context in which the experience occurs. You get wired up with internal chemicals; it is possible to interpret the feelings as fireworks of fun or fire-bombs of fear depending on the surroundings and your expect-ations.

Arousal is a term psychologists use to talk about the gen-eral state that occurs when our bodies are revved up. Fear is just one type of arousal. You can refer to the first part of the article for the description of what fear entails physiologically. In gen-eral, arousal includes any kind of excitement, sexual reactions, aggression, anger, sadness, joy, or exhilaration. Exhilaration is where the fireworks are enjoyable, terror is where they start threatening us.

The typical psychological model for this is the "inverted U", meaning too little arousal leads to boredom, while at some intermediate point the arousal is at an optimum level – we're ex-cited and focused – and as the level of arousal ratchets upward, it becomes more aversive. Anxiety distracts us, then starts suffoca-ting and consuming us, until we reach fear or even terror. As an illustration of this idea, think of the famous quote about war that sums up the two extremes: "war: mind-numbing boredom broken by short bursts of abject terror." There isn't any "optimal arous-al" in war.

The reason we use a general term like arousal, is that many of our emotions are almost exactly the same physiology-ically. It is difficult to tell them apart by the chemistry or intern-al responses. For example, the same general physiological re-sponses occur in fear as occur in anger, and even in excitement. This speaks to the complexity of human learning. A major part of any emotional reaction comes from the meaning the situation has for us. So our experience of one emotion – or its opposite – it is largely due to what we see as context. Being out of control on a roller coaster ride is great fun for a teenager, but it may be a traumatic disaster for a child. Deliberately swimming a Class II rapid and catching eddies like an otter is an absolute blast, but for a beginning kayaker, dumping unexpectedly in the same rapid, choking and bailing out can be utterly terrifying. We differentiate according to context, and interpretation can mean the difference between a great experience and a horrible one. A nice example is another friend who responded the exactly opposite of Steve. He swam repeatedly on every run of his first season, freezing, shivering, and getting bruised, but he thought it was fun and never felt afraid.

A more dramatic example is when the same place evokes both extremes. I experienced this one of the first times I paddled the Lochsa river in the early 1980s. The Lochsa is one of the world's great class III+/IV play rivers, it's big water, with big holes and waves and fantastic drops for 35 miles. However, it was considered serious territory back then, particularly for mere intermediates. We came over with huge anticipation, worried but resolved to run it. We were intermediates who felt right on the cusp of a world-defining challenge.

My two partners and I were in flimsy 13-foot fiberglass boats, and after some sobering rapids, we were just trying to get down the river without getting trashed. It had been cloudy the entire time, and then started raining heavily. The river looked dark and foreboding. We'd managed to survive most of the run, but were close to our limit when we came down on a dramatic drop and confronted a monstrous crashing wave. We eddied out and talked it over. There was lots of tense gesturing and speculation. One friend was really scared and said, "It's going to rip us out of our boats. I'm cold and tired. I'm getting out. Right here. Right now." The other friend said, "It's too big, it's going to break our boats in half."

As they started climbing out, the sun came out and showed brightly and warmly. Suddenly, all the foreboding was gone. The river looked clean and sparkling and beautiful.

I had a welter of feelings. I was worried and on the verge of getting out too. But I'd been having a good time, and now the sunlight completely changed the mood and I found myself saying, "Other people have run the thing. It must be possible." I gritted my teeth and headed down, tensing up as I got nearer and nearer, then confronted the wave looming over me. I remember thinking, "Oh my god, I'm wrong - this thing is *huge*..." It picked up the kayak and flipped me over backwards end for end, and I somehow came surfing down the front face of the wave. My eyes bugged wide open, the world careened wildly by. Reflexly, I managed two cutbacks with the boat skipping and bouncing, and then the wave broke on me and I submarined out.

First thought: *Wow, I made it!* Second thought: *We can surf the thing!* The wave was massive and intimidating – thick, totally clear, and towering over our heads. It would undulate smoothly and then occasionally lift up and collapse with a deep *thump*, then smooth out again. We discovered we could actually get back up to it with a little scraping over the rocks, and all three of us tentatively tried some more surfs, getting the thrill of our lives. There were no broken boats. No being ripped out of the cockpit. Just wild rides in crystal clear water with the sun pouring down and the canyon glistening in a million shades of green. We surfed for three hours and one friend swam after getting beaten down by the break, but we slapped each other and laugh-ed and shouted again and again, "This is the *best* river in the whole damn world!! This is the *best* surf wave on the whole damn planet!"

After that, it was the first place we went to surf. It's call-ed "Pipeline."

That shows the whole sweep of emotions is right there any time, from fear to exhilaration. It shows that in a few minutes you can run out across the inverted "U" from optimal arousal to worry to terror and back to ecstasy. It's all in how you interpret the context.

These last examples suggest another important fact about arousal. People differ immensely in how reactive they are to events. Some people seem frightened by everything; others don't seem to get upset no matter what. Some people are impulsive and love new experiences, others are cautious, and still others are terrified by novelty and change. Such differences may have roots in upbringing and prior experiences that don't have anything directly to do with rivers or water, and people also seem to be geared differently in their basic responses to the world. When you couple these individual differences in reactivity to the effects of context, it means in a group of people you can expect the entire universe of possible experiences. It also means that there is no one description or solution that will apply to all people and all situations.

Exploration as a primal motive?

While I stressed above that psychologically we're geared to be cautious for survival, I have to add here that at the other extreme, testing limits and exploring might be a primal motivation that can override fear. Just as people have huge variations in their arousal, they vary greatly in how they respond to the unknown, and how willing they are to take risks. It's a fact about the world that sometimes great discoveries can be made by those who decided to look where others feared to tread. As maybe the most dramatic example of this, think about the tribes in Siberia who somehow decided to head north into the unknown, crossed the land bridge to the new world and found two entire continents full of mountain ranges, huge lakes, deserts, and vast prairies filled with unknown threats and wonders. They could have stayed on familiar ground, but instead they engaged in one of the greatest acts of exploration in the history of humankind. So I personally believe probing the unknown must be an important part of our humanity, even if it's only done in very small steps by each of us individually. I felt it strongly that first day on the Lochsa, and many times since. I'm equally sure every reader has felt it too, on other runs, and in other parts of your lives. I think this is also why a great adventure epic both raises the hair on our heads, and inspires us. Every emotion is intimately interwoven with its opposite.

***

Fear in Kayaking: Part Three – Controlling Fear

This is the third and final part of our discussion of fear in kayaking. In the first part we discussed the physiology of fear. It is a hard wired reaction to threats and an essential part of our ability to survive, creating a flood of physiological fireworks that overwhelm conscious action and tend to keep us safe despite ourselves. The problem faced by kayakers is that these reactions evolved to work on land, and readily lead to disaster in moving water.

The second part discussed the psychology of fear and how excitement can change into fear or vice versa, depending on our interpretation of a situation. It also discussed how quickly and powerfully we can learn to fear almost anything, and that what is learned in one instant of fear can last our entire life. Fear a serious emotion that can shackle us even when it is a completely unrealistic reaction. These ideas lead us to the psychology of controlling fear.

Proactive basics

One of the cognitive effects of fear is that the emotion takes over before you can have any conscious thought. Rational decision making is left far behind, struggling with tunnel vision, trying in vain to catch up to the freight train that's been let loose, or command the paralyzed legs that refuse to move.

How do you deal with this? The best way is <u>proactively</u>, doing everything you can to prepare yourself solidly so you are less likely to be thrown out of control and feel threatened to begin with. Greater competence, control, skill and understanding are the best way to deal with fear – because they allow you to avoid it in the first place. Here's a quick list of proactive basics before we go into specifics.

Get in decent physical condition. If you are out of shape, you are asking for problems. You will find everything easier if you are fit, strong and have good cardio conditioning.

When choosing rivers and types of paddling, the mantra is, **take small steps**. Do your best to stay within your ability and stretch it carefully. It is very easy to overreach in kayaking and quickly find yourself in the middle of some ugly experience. Taking smaller steps minimizes that chance while also expanding your experience.

Build your skills systematically ALL the time, working on weaknesses and improving strengths. This shouldn't be some long and onerous list of things – it represents all the fun you get to have while learning the sport. It means improving both physical skills and mental skills. The physical skills are all the standard techniques in paddling – cruising, touring, playpaddling, river running, and slalom. They should be done in as many types of water as possible: rivers and creeks big and small, steep and gentle. And do not shy from lakes and the ocean, as they also have their challenges and pleasures for skills. I recommend paddling as many different kinds of boats as you can buy, beg or borrow – creek boats, play boats, big water boats, slalom and squirt boats, C-1, open canoes, downriver racing kayaks, touring boats, and sea kayaks. Every single one of these will teach you something important. This is also a fun range of things you can do over one or multiple seasons as the runoff or rains or drought change water levels. You don't need whitewater to work on many important skills, or on your basic conditioning and paddle strokes. The general approach is: use whatever water and craft you have available and paddle as much as you can and enjoy.

For whitewater, the skills that keep you safe have to replace or redirect your instinctive survival reflexes, because they are the only things that can deal with the dynamics of the river. This means you have to learn those skills very, very well. How well? As an example, look at one standard skill that deserves special mention – a "combat roll". The classic situation is missing a must-make roll right above a drop or when you're tired and distracted. The solution? Learning to mastery.

Learn to mastery – combat roll

I know every one of you has at some point dumped, found yourself upsidedown and trying to roll, feeling that the end of the world is just downstream. In that situation almost inevitably we panic and rush the roll. The predictable result is either we don't make it up and suffer the consequences, or we struggle and feel like we made it by the skin of our teeth. Both outcomes provoke a feeling of insecurity and we start doubting our ability. This is the genesis of fear.

Saying somebody has a combat roll is just a statement that their roll is solid, and they can do it under pressure. My point is, when you've learned it right your regular roll *is* a combat roll. It should be dependable, consistent, and strong. You should be able to crank it off from any angle, no matter where the paddle is. It's unlikely that many of you can do that, and if so, this indicates you have not learned it well enough. The solution: keep practicing, keep analyzing it, and shoot for perfection. Learn to mastery.

The way to approach this is to assume you have never learned your roll well enough, and to continually be working on it. Got a roll on one side? Learn it on the other. Learn how to do it sweeping backward or forward on both sides. Fall over with the paddle on one side, feather the paddle around and roll up on the other side. Throw the paddle away, learn a hands roll both sides, going forward and backward. Having trouble rolling in turbulence? Find a benign eddyline and practice rolling up in no-man's land. You'll quickly realize that you have to be aware of which way the water is going relative to your sweep – if you sweep with the current you won't get any lift, but if you simply hold the paddle at a lifting angle the current will provide the force; if you then supply the hips, you'll pop right up. Try whirlpools. Keep going, and never stop practicing. Never assume that you've got it down and can simply rely on it, because that's just the time when the river will throw a curve at you.

Remember, it's not just a technical skill you learn once and then know, it also requires **constant training** for stamina, strength, and timing. Depending on how and where you paddle, you probably will have to do it when you're tired, cold, out of breath, or even hurt, so you should always train and strengthen it, making it more powerful and more efficient. Treating it this way has probably saved my life more than once. Over the last 25 years, I've rolled up in the middle of manic class V with broken ribs, a dislocated collarbone, dislocated and separated shoulders, and various other maladies. I just assume that my roll is never good enough, and continue to work on it to this day. This is obsessive from most people's standpoints, and admittedly it is aimed toward dealing with the highest end runs, but I've found myself very impressed with how dynamic and powerful the world's rivers are, and it's simply foolish to take even an "easy" river for granted.

Of course, you don't need to go to this extreme, but the same approach works to provide you a virtually fail-safe roll for long play days, or when you're distracted, tired, or even if you're hurt. Pursue the idea of training your roll as a strength and endurance skill, and you'll find it vastly improved. With that comes increased confidence, increased fun, and a sense of freedom. To the limit of your time and motivation, **apply this to all your rivers skills** - learn all of them to mastery. Real, demonstrated control is the best defense against fear.

Proactive mental skills

It is actually wrong to separate physical and mental skills, because both come into play any time you're on the river. The discussion here is for convenience and it somewhat artificially stresses one or the other – so please understand that kayaking always requires their synthesis. Realistically, all mental skills have to be backed up by physical skills, and vice versa. I would say that mental skills might typically include tenacity, toughness, focus, keeping cool, but there are more specific ones as well, such as learning to read whitewater, scout, understand a line and how to stay on it, and judgment about what a river requires and whether you are up to it. I must add that the most important mental skill you can possess is judgment, and specifically the ability to be honest with yourself about what you feel. The best practice for all of them is lots of paddling in as many circumstances and rivers as you can – again taking small steps.

Three versions of a core mental skill

It's useful to consider three ideas that are closely tied together. They are so general they could even be called attitudes rather than skills, and actually, each has elements of all the mental skills I listed above. They are: not rushing, focus under pressure, and keeping your cool. All of them assume you might be feeling threatened and even fearful, but you are not allowing that to degrade your paddling. Not rushing emphasizes the physical movements a bit more, and that you maintain effective technique and timing for your skills. Focus emphasizes something a bit more mental - that even if you are feeling fear, you continue to deal with the situation in a clear and effective way. Both of them assert that you can't allow an impending threat to screw up your technique or problem solving. The phrase, "keeping cool under fire" expresses something a little more general, of not allowing yourself to be shanghaied by threat or fear. Obviously, it leads to the same end of not rushing and keeping your focus. I don't want to play with words here, but only acknowledge that they are overlapping ideas people commonly talk about. Each of them suggests a slightly different emphasis on what skills you need to build.

The proactive approach to this group of mental skills is to learn your techniques so well that even when you have to make a split-second decision, your response is sharp and effective, properly timed, and your technique does not falter. Further, that level of learning allows you to keep problem-solving effectively, not get distracted, or sucked into tunnel vision. Of course all these things are easy to say but difficult to do, so consider this a principle that you work toward.

All three skills assert the same basic fact: no matter how close you feel you are to disaster, you cannot give in to fear or allow yourself to be distracted by it. You must always focus on what has to be done, and do it. The instant you rush, lose focus, or lose your cool, you have given up your control to the river. The following two contrasting examples illustrate this principle.

A few months ago on boatertalk, a guy described a very ugly swim through several rapids on the Green. He flipped, panicked, rushed a roll and missed it, bailed out of his boat and tried to swim to shore. He didn't make the eddy, was swept over a rocky drop and slammed his head, broke out teeth and got a concussion. He was helped by a number of people and made it out, however, he's got a hefty dentist's bill, a sore head, and he's going to have some major fear lurking in his feelings about that river, that drop, his roll, and his general confidence about paddling. One instant and some major consequences. His description was precise so it sounded like once he swam, he was thinking clearly. I don't want to sound like Dr. Second Guess, but from the perspective here, that clarity would have been far better used staying in his boat, keeping his focus and cool, not rushing, and hitting his roll. Fear pushed him to react outside of his paddling technique, which as we've emphasized before, leads to a fight or flight reaction that is almost always dangerous on the river. It's good that his river computer kicked in, and it shows he had the ability to focus, but critically, it wasn't applied within his paddling skills. The river computer booted up because once swimming he knew he had no other options. I would emphasize that once you're out of your boat you have given the river every advantage there is, and you're left with very few options and very little control. I believe the situation illustrates many of the principles we've talked about.

The second example is somewhat the opposite end of the spectrum. Twenty-some years ago on the first descent of a fantastic steep creek in North Idaho – 600+ feet per mile of waterslides and boulderfields – I ran a big complex slide and got stuffed in the nasty hole at the bottom. A friend tossed a throw rope while I was windowshading and cartwheeling, and it unraveled all around me in the hole. I had loops around my neck, paddle, arms, and waist. The rope drag pulled me out of the hole and I had perhaps ten seconds across a fast moving pool to roll up and untangle myself before entering a nasty Class V+ rapid. Needless to say, entering a class V+ rapid with a noose around your neck trailing a throw rope is not a good idea. In fact, it has death written all over it. I cranked a roll, felt the rope strands all around me, and started untangling myself. My brain screamed at me as I watched the oncoming rapid out of the corner of my eye, while calmly and deliberately unwrapping each loop, right to the last instant with the current accelerating me into the first must-make move. I cast off the last loop and already had angled my boat for the drop, making the move and scrabbling into an eddy. Only then did I realize how heavily I was breathing. The friend who threw the rope was mortified, although I don't blame him because he was doing was seemed right at the time. We laughed about it later, but nearly killing me is still a sore spot with him all these years later. He should get over it.

The point: you absolutely cannot lose your head and you cannot rush things. You must stay calm and deal with the problem as required, improvising and keeping effective decisions coming - regardless of the looming threat. Control and focus are the only things that keep you safe. The instant you lose your cool, you have thrown away your best chance to come through safely. Your fear has won and you are likely to be the loser. The only question left is, how bad is it going to be?

Reality Training

Once fear has taken hold, it is a huge internal battle to get your control back. If the situation lasts for a little while, say more than 10, 15 or 20 seconds, you probably can catch your balance. The problem is, an awful lot can happen on the river in 10 or 20 seconds. Again, the best thing is to have very well learned skills, optimally they would be proactively practiced in a similar situation.

In the martial arts, there are dozens of "reality based" self-defense schools that are set up to put people in high-octane situations to train their skills, so they react correctly under pressure. Typically one or more attackers are geared up in scary looking paddled suits and you go through a set of scenarios – an attempted mugging, robbery, car jacking, or attack with a knife, and the person can freely use the most aggressive of defense techniques. What typically happens is that under pressure, all the fine points of technique disappear and the only things left are gross motor movements and primal emotion. It's a real eye-opener to anybody who thinks he or she will clobber the attacker like Claude VanDamme does in the movies with that cool-looking roundhouse kick. It won't happen. The practice scenarios lead to focusing on the critical aspects: keeping control of fear, making clear decisions based on a few principles of safety, and using simple, effective techniques. The key point is to experience as close as possible the same emotions and stress – but safely – as in a real situation. Having practiced it, you can hone in on just a few effective actions and not be paralyzed with fear. Once you have practiced the responses, you then have a chance to control fear, or fight through it while effectively defending yourself.

I don't recommend you deliberately scare yourself on the river. However, you can do the same general kind of "reality-based" training with kayaking, mostly because kayaking is fully "reality-based" all by itself. Running rivers generally gives us plenty of situations for proactive mental practice under some pressure. It's the inherent nature of the river situation. Again, use small steps. Even on your local play run you can set up moves that are difficult and require careful attention and control. Also, practice swimming rapids, getting a throw rope to a swimmer, using a z-drag to peel a broached boat off logs or boulders in the current. Prepare as much as possible. You can call it preparation, but really it's also a lot of fun.

Yet another training situation is competition. It is not quite the same kind of pressure, but it can induce stress and mild fear from knowing you have one chance, especially when racing slalom, competing in freestyle or downriver racing. This allows you to practice focus and control when feeling mild fear.

The problem is there are no consequences so the emotions are not the same. It is self-imposed competitive anxiety and not a feeling evoked by a fundamental threat to your safety. A perfect example of the difference was a National Team/World Cup slalom racer who started doing hard runs with some friends of mine on the west coast. The guy was a very, very good technical paddler and I have the utmost respect for his skills. However, on one particular run there was an awkward, tight move right in front of an ugly log that spanned the main current. It was a serious Class V+ situation. Missing the move looked like death. After two members made the drop, the slalom paddler dismissed all suggestions for what to do and headed down. He missed the move, froze in the instant he had to react, and simply stared at the oncoming log. Crashing broadside into it, he flipped and was sucked under as my friends went into rescue mode. He was trapped deep underwater for several seconds, then the boat launched completely out of the water on the backside of the log. He rolled up and caught an eddy, whitefaced with eyes wide. Summarizing the situation, my friend Rick said, "If that boy is going to paddle with us much more, he needs to develop a better panic stroke."

That's typical humor for Rick. His comment underscores that in truly serious situations on the river, there can be no hesitation - you must react. Particularly in Class V you may have only an instant and every shred of your emotion has to be channeled into the one thing that will save you. If you miss a move in such a situation, staring at the log that is about to kill you doesn't get the job done. Note that in this case the kayaker was completely within his physical skills – in fact, he was without question the most highly skilled technical paddler on the river that day. But he didn't have the mindset that would allow his skills to save him when he missed a move he assumed he would make.

While it perhaps comes out most strikingly in hard whitewater, this lesson applies at every level of the sport. A direct, clear response is essential regardless of whether you are in class I or class V. It is not a question of difficulty; it is a question of being able to focus and act.

The way to practice this is to make moves in everything from easy to more challenging rapids. Gradually work your way up according to whatever your desire for challenge is. The problem with the paddler above was that he'd done tens of thousands of extremely hard kayaking moves on slalom courses, but didn't have the fundamental feeling of consequences. When suddenly faced with it, he froze, which if you remember is a perfect example of an instinctive fear response that you cannot allow on a river. The ability to make an instantaneous decision with complete commitment defines what river running requires as much as any physical or technical skill does.

Managing fear once you have it

Fear ruins your appreciation of the sport. It makes paddling into an aversive experience instead of the fun it should be. Please don't accept it as a fact of life on the river. If you are fearful of kayaking but still want to paddle, get some help and acquire the skills that make being on the river one of the best experiences you can have.

There are a number of standard ways to work with fear, as developed in various therapies.

First, when you feel fear creeping through you, **learn how to relax and calm down**. One effective method is deliberately breathing more slowly and deeply, and from your abdomen rather than from your chest. At the same time, systematically learn to relax all the muscles in your body. You can learn to cue and practice these things as a skill; using specific imagery and music or sounds to reinstate relaxation. Practice enough so you can do it right there on the river. A great many high level athletes in other sports do this for competitions. There are courses in which this is taught as a technique for dealing with anxiety.

Replace unrealistic fearful thoughts with realistic constructive thoughts. Take control of your visualization. Often fear takes this over and your imagination is set loose in the service of your fear. It takes conscious will power, practice, and attention to reverse this. The same thing can be done with positive imagery about what will happen, which is closely allied to the modeling I mentioned above. Again, there are many formal courses and ways to learn this.

Systematically desensitize yourself by gradual exposure to aspects of the fearful situation, done under control – *safely* – and carefully, until you no longer feel the same intense reactions. This is a typical method used with phobias and will work better for unrealistic fears than realistic ones.

If you've had problems, **take a step back, or two or three steps, build skills back up** carefully using the kind of approach I mentioned above. All the things I mentioned in prior pages about practicing and building skills apply here. These increase your ability to cope with situations, understand, and be able to control them. It is the direct way and probably the most effective in the long run.

Use transfer of training. For desensitizing and stepping back, look around on your local rivers and find simple features that have some of the elements that give you trouble, and work to develop skill, understanding and control. If you have trouble with balance or rolling on eddylines, pick a strong eddyline with a pool below and work your roll. If you're scared of holes, find a small hole or breaking surfwave with a big eddy below. What you're doing is approximating the more difficult river experience. It's called transfer. You learn a skill in one situation and apply it in another. The better learned it is, the better the transfer. This is true for both physical and mental skills. Doing it in a simpler setting allows you to gain the control needed to avoid fear.

Get support. Find friends who you can talk to and are willing to work through it with you. You'll probably find that many of them have similar problems.

Don't let other paddlers, even if they are friends, goad you into bad decisions. Especially don't paddle with people who think it's funny when somebody screws up and gets blasted, because at some point it'll be you. It's much better to find people who will support each other instead of people projecting their insecurities onto others.

Don't run rapids you're afraid of. If you build your skills carefully there will come a time when it makes sense to you to run something. There's no need to hurry the process. Impatience increases the likelihood of overreaching and having bad experiences.

Something I would strongly suggest NOT to do is use pot or tranquillizers or some other drug. If you need them to control your anxiety, then you're trying to cover up some serious problems in the wrong way.

Avoid macho attitudes. The guys who paddle because they see it as a macho thing are often – not always – fearful right underneath the bravado. If you are somebody who feels this macho attitude, I suggest you think really carefully about what you're trying to get from the sport. It has far more satisfying rewards than stroking your manhood, and the latter need is almost guaranteed to lead to a poor decision at some point.

Listen carefully to your own inner voices and feelings. Do what is right for you. Those inner voices reflect your intuition, which is an awareness that goes far beyond anything you can consciously identify. It is the sum of your personal experience and reflects everything you sense at the time. As you gain additional experience, your intuition will change because it always reflects your knowledge, and equally, the limitations of that knowledge. Bring it into your awareness.

Find your own balance. It doesn't have to be anybody else's. There's no reason to try and do class IV or V. If you feel compelled to try, then make as sure as possible you are prepared.

This last thing deserves a special comment. Our videos and magazines glorify the most outrageous and difficult runs, which gives people the impression that to be a real kayaker you have to run 80-foot waterfalls or gnarly Class V. That is bullshit. The only rule about kayaking is having fun. It doesn't matter at what level. I love being out on the water – any water – and I'm per-fectly happy paddling on a lake or in Class I with beginners as I am paddling harder rivers. The quality of the experience is what I look for, and a good partner is not just somebody who does hard runs with you, it's anybody you can share an enjoyable time with on a river. If difficulty led to insight, wisdom, or satis-faction, then all the class V paddlers out there would be wise gurus, fully satisfied with all they have done. I assure you they aren't. They are a wide assortment of characters with every sort of quirk, anxiety, and fetish. Skill level by itself doesn't mean anything except the person has done a lot of paddling. My suggestion is, no matter what your level and no matter what you paddle, it's your thoughtfulness on and off the river that defines your path. There is no reason to hurry along a beautiful path; there is every reason to savor it.

Find the joy! The positive experiences are what draw us to rivers, the pleasure and sheer fun of moving with water, seeing the beauty of the river, and being with good friends. Weave your sense of the river out of the joy you have in dis-covering and learning, and it will become a deep well you can draw from.

Ways to put it all together

Paddling requires blending all the physical and mental skills together. This is what defines the overall skill of white-water kayaking. The following things should help integrate all the points we've mentioned here.

Modeling: No matter what your skill level, strive for grace and smoothness in moving down the river. The smoother you are, the more efficient and effective your paddling is. If you are struggling, then you're doing something wrong. Watch other good paddlers. Play close attention in videos to the techniques and moves they use. Feel yourself into that motion. A good internal image of a perfect run will make you a better paddler. Actually getting there may be a long-term process of improving skills, but having a vividly imagined goal of how you want to paddle makes it clear what you need to do. Even videotape yourself. There's nothing like an objective third person point of view to see what you are doing. It doesn't have to be in whitewater, even a few minutes of seeing yourself flatwater paddling will teach you a great deal. Most likely, you'll find the damnedest little hitches and irregularities, you'll be surprised and horrified you because you'll look like a spazz. That's good, don't be self-conscious, just use it for motivation, correct errors, and improve.

Focus drills. An important mental skill for river running is quickly deciding and making a particular move. There are some simple ways to practice this, which require you to rivet your attention on exactly what you're going to do and how it will be done. Depending on your skill level, you should make the move challenging by making the window of opportunity small, which mimics more difficult lines in whitewater. As paddling gets harder, those little windows get smaller and there are more of them stacked back to back. Class III assumes you have to control your line down the river within a certain limit, which might be moving to miss a single hole or rock. Class IV really assumes that you have several such moves and the consequences of missing them is substantial. Class V assumes that there are multiple difficult moves with small margins of error and severe consequences.

Slalom gates on easy whitewater are a great way to practice this aspect of planned, focused movement. You have to identify and plan out what needs to be done – which is a general skill that comes into play in all whitewater. It might be only a simple eddy move, but you will find that with the gate there, suddenly you have to be just in the right place or else you can't do it. Without the gates, you will never realize how sloppy and uncontrolled you are. And they show you that without harsh consequences. Entering a foot too high means you hit one of the poles. Better slapping into a slalom gate than slamming into a rock. Or, the gate itself may be set low in an eddy, forcing you to crowd the gate, because entering too low may get you swept out of the eddy behind. If you think that's contrived, well, I know of two people who nearly died when they hit eddies too low and were fed into sieves in class IV drops. Slalom teaches you not to be lazy about your moves, and trust me, that attitude will come in handy.

Downstream gates are especially important. A simple sequence of three offset downstream gates will demonstrate to you how difficult it is to move laterally across the current, and exactly what is required to accomplish it (quickly changing your boat angle, backpaddling or even turning into an upstream ferry angle). You have to be able to control these if you are going to paddle confidently and sharply even in Class III whitewater. They are essential in anything beyond that. If you can't do it, then you've got some major holes in your skills. Such sequences also give you extremely useful knowledge about how to read lines in a rapid, how to think about the current and your boating skills, and it will help you interpret river features that you may never have paid any attention to in the past. Finally, it will force you to look at the water <u>between</u> the key moves, which in turn integrates your strokes and angles into your thinking about how to get from one place to another. This will spur a growing awareness about how all parts of the river are connected, and what you need to do to follow a particular line. That awareness unfolds with practice and will leave you with a very different appreciation of how beautiful the river is. The more refined your awareness and ability, the more pleasure the river can give you. Each such increment in your focus and skill is a step toward greater control and less fear.

Find and practice flow

Running whitewater is both intuitive and analytic. The analysis is comprised of all the technique you've trained and all the explicit decisions you've made. The intuitive realm is where it all comes together, culminating in the feeling of blending with the water. All the basic skills for balance, controlling direction and speed, reading ahead, must be integrated into your feeling of the flowing water. It's both a beautiful experience and the way you do it amounts to your style of paddling.

Flow should be practiced at each stage, each level of difficulty, and with each individual rapid. As the difficulty of the whitewater increases, keeping a nice flowing style is dramatically harder, because each of the skills must be that much better learned and integrated together, but the process is the same at any level from class I to class VI. The best way to practice this is on rivers well within your abilities. They should probably be at least one or two grades below your maximum, places where your timing is not forced and not so powerful that your strength is overwhelmed. Develop your sense of a nice flowing line, running in control. This is tremendously enjoyable and it is perhaps the greatest overall skill. As you develop, you can bootstrap yourself up by dealing with faster and more powerful rivers to whatever level you have the skills and desire to take on. But at each level you need to feel yourself into the flow. Every time you feel this, it will both be excellent practice, and also remind you why you love paddling.

What kayaking is not: Psychological theories of "sensation seeking" and "adrenaline rushes"

You should use anything that helps you, but I would caution paddlers about using books talking about risk. In psychological research, fear and risk are talked about in a number of different theories, such as "sensation seeking", "thrill seeking", "risky behavior", "reversal theory", "Type A+ theory", and others. I'm not going to discuss them because frankly, I have not found these theories to be of much help in understanding kayaking or any of the other adventure sports I've done. Each makes incorrect assumptions, which I believe is because their originators were armchair academics and laboratory researchers rather than doers. They were people who never had any direct experience and do not understand the nature of the sports. Typically, they focus on surface characteristics, for example equating whitewater kayaking with riding a roller coaster or bungee jumping. As one simple difference, the roller coaster and bungee jumping require no skill at all because you have no control over the outcome. Nothing you do affects it. You are a passive participant and put your life into the hands of people you typically don't know, and are passively controlled by equipment whose quality and properties you can't assess. In contrast, the entire purpose of paddling a kayak is to actively control one's path down a river and interact with the water's flow. The researchers make the mistake of assuming the psychology of passive recipients is the same as that of willful, learning, active agents. That's one primary reason why I'm not using them to describe any aspect of fear in kayaking.

Last words

Kayaking is capable of tweaking just about every phobia that any of us could ever have; it is likewise capable of giving us the most rewarding and moving experiences. Fear focuses on the dark side of the unknown, while mystery and inspiration focus on the light and beautiful side. Fear speaks to the dark threats hidden in the water and within ourselves. It can take the simple and powerful form of claustrophobia or of being trapped inside the kayak. Of being upsidedown not able to breathe. Of being swept away by forces we can't control into some unknown disaster lurking downstream. The horizonline is both a metaphor and a reality - you can't see what is ahead as the roar of the rapid gets louder and louder. It's the very thing that every movie director uses to evoke tension and get us on the edge of our seats. The hint of something bad, growing stronger and stronger, tension increasing, every primitive reflex becomes engaged, sight, sound, all by suggestion of threat and evoking a sense of dread. It's not necessary to see any gore; our emotions can be completely driven by an impending sense of threat.

It is within our power to shift all these from threats to beautiful possibilities. Awe comes when our emotions speak to the positive. Then, the horizonline becomes the doorway to challenge, fun, and unfolding opportunity. When we make that shift, all the hints, potential threats, and darkness turn to their mirror images on the positive side. This is fully within our power.

Mystery and inspiration come from the same place fear does - from confronting something larger than ourselves, from reaching the brink of our understanding and not knowing what is beyond. You cannot ban one of those emotions without banning the others. Somebody who narrows his world in order to control it at all costs will end up stifling mystery. He will feel barriers instead of sensing possibilities. He will feel weakened instead of strengthened.

Fear is a shackle. It prevents us from seeing that we can almost always do far more than we think. Left to itself, it stymies our abilities, and gives us a false sense that the world is smaller than it really is, and that our skills are less than they really are or can be. Fear narrows our thinking, our relationship to the world and to ourselves. It is like the inverse of imagination. It is our creativity turned in a direction that hinders rather than helps us.

This is why the river is such a magnificent symbol, and why kayaking is such an incredible sport. It projects us into a different world where comfort and familiarity are taken away, and where we have to learn completely new skills. That world opens up in beauty and complexity, and at the same time it unveils our inner world and attitudes – weaknesses that we never knew we had, and strengths that we never thought we could attain.

The river is a fountain of inspiration. Fleetingly, it gives us the experience of flowing effortlessly and leaves us with a glimpse of perfection. It is precisely in striving toward that sense of flowing perfection that our sport becomes such a wonderful game, a satisfying pleasure, a serious challenge, and a life passion. Whitewater kayaking is the ultimate flow sport, giving us the keys to balance solidity and change, reality and imagination. In that tension and release lie the riches of the world.

***

Interview with www.SteepCreek.com

Author's note: This is not a formal essay. However, I was asked a series of interview questions by Ben Friberg, who runs www.steepcreek.com, and the answers dwell on a number of topics that fit "whitewater philosophy." The format leads to a different kind of approach to the ideas. I hope readers find them of interest.

What is your personal taste in kayaks?
I started out in 13-foot fiberglass boats in the 1970s and have paddled everything down to six-foot playboats. Every boat and every design has its place. It will do certain things and not others. There are plenty of good boats out there, and I don't get hung up on the details. A good paddler should have the skill to make the best out of anything he or she is in, know what its strengths are and be able to use them, and also what its limitations are and how to compensate for them.

What kind of rescue gear do you have? On a serious run, all the standard things: carabiners, two pulleys, a good rope (!), prussiks, webbing. One absolute: never paddle without a throw rope. My friends Eric Nies and Brennan Guth did that and Brennan died because of it, but it just as well could have been Eric. Don't assume nothing will happen, even on class II. The river is full of things that can happen. The life you save will be your friend's, and the life they save will be yours. At its best the sport is a deep celebration of all that life can give. Dying while you're celebrating life is perhaps the most contradictory and futile thing possible.

What is your preference for paddles? I have the same comment as for boats. Try everything and understand how it works. I used an Illiad paddle when I started — a huge battle-ax of a thing. I used wooden Nimbus paddles, the early Werner paddles, Harmony, Lightning, and a host of others. You should have the skill to adapt to any gear. Bent shafts are a fad, not a necessity. Likewise with asymmetrical blades. They have small ergonomic benefits, but I have yet to see anything done with a bent shaft or an asymmetrical blade that couldn't be done without one. Overall, I don't like preferences. The thing that preferences do is make you somewhat more rigid about interacting with the river, which to me is the opposite of what the river teaches. It teaches fluidity and continual, effortless adaptation to everything. I take that simple truth as my ideal.

<u>What are your favorite creeks</u>? I am a paddler and creeking is only one part of paddling, so I can't answer strictly in terms of creeks. That would be like trying to write using only five letters of the alphabet. Believe it or not, one of my favorites is the local Class II – III Blackfoot River. People get so locked into class V and waterfalls that they forget the beauty of the water, which is why I'm on the river in the first place. If you can't get pleasure out of the act of paddling no matter where that is, then you should think carefully about your motives. As far as harder runs, there are dozens of steep creeks nearby, and I've run god-knows how many thousands of class V and VI rapids. They are interesting, but they are not the sum of the sport. One of my all-time favorites will remain nameless. I've run it a number of times and to my knowledge nobody else has ever found it. It's in a deep quartzite gorge, has multiple waterfalls 20 to 35 feet, long cascades, an interesting roped portage around a cascading sieve, and a mile of biggish water class V at the end. It's all of paddling in a nutshell, and nobody else knows about it even after all these years. Oh, and I like Smith Creek up in the Idaho panhandle too – great multiple runs on it and upper tributaries, steep granite waterslides, punchbowl falls at the end; very classy. Lion Creek creek is great too. We did the first descent in 1990, and my favorite drop was one of the steep slides where my friend Paul Kopczynski had to shinny about 50 or 60 feet up a cedar tree to photograph the run. It was maybe 1200 feet per mile - so steep

there wasn't any place to shoot from and see what the rapid was doing.

<u>Name five cities for creeking</u>: I love western Montana and wouldn't live anyplace else. Don't mind visiting, but I like these big mountains and rivers with great bakeries, friends from grade school and high school, plenty of options for kayaking, good music scene. I can step out my door and in a few minutes be hiking on any of four or five different mountains. It's three minutes to the river, and another minute to Brennan's wave. 15 minutes to the Blackfoot.

<u>Playboats on steep creeks</u>. I'll almost never tell anybody not to do something, even if I think it's really unadvisable. Personal freedom is a big part of paddling, and if somebody wants to use a playboat on a steep creek, that's okay – except if I'm on the team. The reason is, one person's poor or inappropriate gear means that other team members may have to compensate or even save him, so in that situation it's a decision that affects the rest of us.

Most boats can be used for most things, but the more specialized the arena, the more care you should take that your equipment fits the situation. In the 80s when squirting came out, people started doing creeks and bigger water in squirt boats. Probably not a great idea, and several people died discovering that it wasn't the tool for the job. Very edgy, no buoyancy, heavy tendency to dive – all bad characteristics for the terrain and all diminish your margin of error. It's worth finding out what the limits of a boat or other gear are, or even your skills – but not worth your life. A young local paddler Max Lentz just died last fall, the son of friends of mine, and it's possible that was partially because he had a play boat that got stuck in a sieve on a creeky line where a bigger boat wouldn't have. A play boat just gives you less leeway for a mistake. I also nearly died once getting trapped between a submerged log and the bottom in the middle of a rapid. If I'd been in a shovel-nosed playboat, I probably would have died. But the river is a place of freedom, and people make personal decisions about what they want to use. Others may disagree, so my choice would be I probably would not paddle with somebody who had a totally inappropriate boat for a run, because I or another team member would likely be the ones trying to save them. But it's a free world, so maybe they'd find somebody else to paddle with. And nobody can see the future, so maybe I'd be the one who got in trouble and the play-boat dude the one who saved me. It's easy to be righteous, and impossible to predict the future.

Differences between creekers and other paddlers:
Paddlers overall are highly individualistic so I wouldn't even try to generalize about their differences. Also, I don't know many people who think of themselves strictly in terms of creeking. I certainly don't think of myself that way, although I've done a large amount of creeking. If I came across somebody strongly self-identified like that, I'd encourage him or her to taste a few of the other fruit our sport has to offer. It's pretty hard to beat surfing on the Lochsa, or doing a trip down the Selway, or padding the Alsek with the massive glaciers and mountains around you. Paddling is a broad and multifaceted sport, filled with beautiful things and places to go. Why limit yourself to one narrow aspect of it?

Is this the Golden Age of kayaking?
I used to think paddling was in a golden age in the 70s and 80s, but we keep finding things, designing new boats that make other things possible, and developing skills. I prefer to think that it will always be developing. I think talk of a "golden age" is nostalgia for a time that hasn't yet occurred and never will.

What is the "Next level"? The sport is always changing and people are always learning and building on what has been done in the past. There will always be a next level no matter where we are now or in the future. The very nature of kayaking is to push what is possible. Blackadar showed what it was possible to do just by daring to try what others thought couldn't be done. People's skills have greatly increased since then, but even now each generation is showing that the limits of the one before were self-imposed, or imposed by equipment, or simply interest and focus. Every generation thinks they're something special, and I suppose they are, but the best of any given era would probably be very good in any other era. So the next levels will keep coming, and I expect in my 80s to be paddling on one of Jupiter's moons.

<u>Do you think creeking is more team oriented than other kinds of paddling?</u>
That depends on the people comprising the team.

<u>East versus West coast runs</u>
There's so much travel back and forth I don't think there's much difference in the paddlers. And there are great runs all over. But there are obvious differences in the quantity of certain types of runs, the size and length of the rivers. Every place has its charm. The Sierras are pretty amazing however, and difficult to match.

<u>Describe an Epic:</u>
I have a skewed view of this. I've always accepted there should be a substantial level of pain and struggle as part of the goal of any trip. If it's less than difficult, I don't like it. However, I reserve "epic" for things like Ernest Shackleton's Antarctic trip in 1914. If you don't know about it, read "Endurance" by Alfred Lansing and you'll understand what a real epic is, and why I use the word sparingly. Most paddling "epics" are milquetoast. Not that they aren't hard or scary or even fatal; it's just that the word is a cliché and isn't used discerningly. Here's a river epic: The Spanish conquistador Aguirre went over the Andes in 1560 and spent a year going down the Amazon river to find the myth-ical El Dorado. They didn't even really know where the river went or how big the continent was. He lost most of his men, repeatedly starved, got malaria, and went crazy. He convinced himself and

his remaining men that he was really the King of the New World, that his daughter was his rightful Queen, and that he was fated to depose the King of Spain and rule the world. Eventually they made it to the coast, constructed ships and sailed back up to Venezuela, then attacked the Spanish base to have Aguirre take his rightful place as King, and were killed. Now that's an epic! What paddling trip could possibly compete with that? And it's why our paddling escapades are milquetoast.

If I survive, I demote the incident to a "mini-epic". Thankfully, I have had a number "mini-epics", such as nearly getting killed, straggling out of the wilderness having shattered my boat, left all my gear, climbed out of some god-forsaken canyon, and been near complete exhaustion. And I've been slammed badly on rivers and weathered near endless pummeling, but fortunately I didn't black out and I survived, so the mini-epics continue. And I have not yet gone crazy, nor do I think I'm going to depose the King of Spain.

Rapids that make me nervous:
I can't answer the question, because this isn't the way I experience rivers. To my mind, if a rapid makes you nervous, then you aren't prepared for it and it's dumb to run it. I run rapids I feel I belong on, and if I don't have that feeling, then I portage. I run rapids if, after I've scouted, I reach a place where I feel like I've been poured right into the river and I'm certain I can do the moves. I wouldn't want to paddle with somebody who was running stuff he was nervous about; it shows bad judgment. There's no way you'll be on top of your game with that weighing you down. My runs have included some very substantial things, and I'd say that the hardest things were not so much steep creeks as high water steep runs, like the NF Payette (especially Jacob's Ladder-Golf Course) at 6000-7000cfs, or Coyote Falls on the SF Clearwater at 5000+. Certain rapids on the Stikine come to mind as very challenging. Those aren't steep creeks, and I can't put any steep creek rapid in their category, even though there are plenty of really mean things that people have run. If you make a

mistake on one of them, you're dead. Steep creeks, even the massive cascades that Steve Fisher was running in Quebec, never have the sense of finality to them that a big river does, especially a river in a deep gorge. They are impressive, obviously dangerous, you surely could get killed on them, but they just don't have the massive gravity. Even ugly, ugly drops on a creek don't have the steely feeling of power and seriousness that you get looking at something like Wasson's Hole on the Stikine at a higher level. There's something about a massive, convulsing volume of water getting stuffed down a huge drop, and the incredible chaotic violence of the surges, that sends shivers up your spine, or when you see huge seams welling and geysering up against the walls, or when the current is so fast that the holes get spun downstream, breaking completely across the river from one wall to the other.

I could say that I was nervous for a little bit when looking at a tape of the Tsangpo Gorge below the confluence with the Po Tsangpo. This was maybe 1997 before any paddler had been in there, and Charlie Munsey and I were looking at a tape he'd gotten from some trekkers. The level must have been 70,000, with huge bedrock waterfalls and rapids and vertical walls at least 500 to 1000 feet high right out of the water. This one drop was probably a 50 or 60-foot waterfall which, because of the level, was an immense shuddering ramp into an apartment-building sized hole. The water was so fast, the hole was exploding straight up into the air. The rapid below it started out with a breaking wave that was probably nearly 20 feet high, and disappeared into offset holes of similar size. The instantaneous thought of being in there was a sharp stick in the gut — fear basically — but it was immediately replaced with laughing at the absurdity of trying to run that stretch in a kayak. We knew looking at it, that no matter who ever went in there, they wouldn't run that drop or anything else remotely like it. It's the biggest whitewater on the planet, but nobody will ever run it.

One other one comes to mind. When we were in Mexico in 1991 we did a movie for *National Geographic* canyoneering the Shumulja River and following it underground. At one place we were a good 700 feet down in a vertical walled gorge, standing on a natural arch about 100 feet above the river, right where it disappeared underground. The river charged over a waterfall, went under the arch, then into this boiling pool, which ended with big whirlpools where the water got sucked under. That sent shivers up your spine, because you were looking at death — but you weren't going to run it. We did a rope traverse across the walls and through a narrow passage, then dropped the boats and ourselves down into the river in the cave system. Read my story "Chen Cave" for the weirdness of it all. There's something about running a river that's 700 feet underground in the jet blackness that is a little disconcerting.

Have you ever lost a close paddling partner?
Yes, over the years about 10 or 12 people, which includes both partners and friends. I feel I'm a ghost, in the sense that you seek for a greater meaning that includes death. The change comes in assessing what the essential worth of paddling is, and what responsibilities you have to yourself and to those who love you, and who are waiting for you at home. If you take those things lightly, or you don't consider them, then you're less human than you should be. I think it's horribly selfish for people to take those risks without considering the serious effects on others. I reject the brain-dead clichés that people spout, like "at least he died doing what he loved," or "that's the price of pushing the envelope." I feel certain that if you could ask the guy while he's dying, he'd say something along the lines of what a waste it was. I know I've felt that after several episodes that I barely got out of. The problem is that most people, and especially younger talented paddlers, cannot understand what it means to die, or to face the emptiness that comes from a close friend dying while doing something that seemed so vibrant and alive. They brush it all away, supremely confident that it won't happen to them or their buddies, but all you have to do is listen to them talk and it's clear they don't comprehend the outcome — the pain, the mean-

inglessness that their parents feel when their energetic, smart child kills himself while playing. There's the glorification of risk, the sense they're engaging in courageous feats facing danger and potential death, laughing at the reaper, but the fantasy collapses when something happens. All the clichés just seem stupid at that point. So I suggest people give all this some careful thought.

Do you solo?
Yes, I soled extensively on hard runs of all kinds for a long period, but don't do it much any more. Names of the places don't matter, although I'm sure at least some readers will know of a couple. The interesting thing is, I'm sure that nearly all serious paddlers solo at some point, mostly because it provides a truly rewarding sense of intimacy with a river. I won't recommend soloing to people, unless they find themselves coming to it for internal reasons, almost despite themselves and without seeking it. On the other end of the spectrum, anybody who solos because he thinks it's cool is fooling himself, mostly because he's defining it socially — which contradicts what it actually means. You do it for the privacy, intimacy, and perhaps for a specific mental and physical challenge. For some people — and I'm thankful to put myself in this group — it can be the most beautiful and rewarding thing imaginable. After many years of aggressive, difficult solos I realized that the difficulty doesn't matter for what I really wanted out of the experience. Certainly the focus and mental challenge are rewarding, the sense of being completely absorbed into a dramatic place. However, soloing just means being alone, so it can be done anywhere. The key element for kayaking is that when you are with other people, even if it's just one other person, paddling is a social experience. But when you are alone, the river itself is your partner. That intimacy with the water is one of the deepest experiences I've ever had, and it took the intensity of the hard runs to fully appreciate it.

Is there a height at which waterfalls become more dangerous? I know good paddlers who have really hurt themselves on falls as low as 20 feet. Depending on the entry and lip and current structure, anything up to 60 or 80 feet seems perfectly controllable. And Tyler Bradt's run on the Slave (107) looked pretty sharp. Felix Lemmler, a Swiss paddler, has done up to 137 feet, but he also hurt himself substantially on one much smaller. I have to say the highest I've ever done is about 55 feet, and I got a concussion on it, so I'm probably not the best guy to ask.

Year started creeking – mid 1980s.

What was your first kayak? My first kayak was a homemade fiberglass boat in about 1973, a takeoff on an obscure Prijon design made by Lynn McAdams, a local fireman who built boats for [Walt] Blackadar. Rob Lesser bought his first boat from Lynn in 1969. I also paddled a Hollowform, and an Eddyline WSL-9, both 13-footers.

When did you first get into kayaking? That depends on how you define "kayak". My family had two foldboats, which was a German two man kayak with a folding internal frame and an outer canvas cover. We paddled on easy local rivers and lakes from the time I was 5 or 6 (about 1962). My older brother bought an Eddyline SL in 1972. I surfed it some in the ocean and went down some of the local runs a couple of times. Also, I was on the swim team and there were kayaks at the pool. When the coach left, we'd pull them up to the high board, get in and launch ourselves off. It was a start.

Who are your heroes?
I don't think of kayakers as heroes. It's just a sport for god's sake. Heroes are people like the Chinese guy in Tiannanmen Square who stood in front of those three tanks and then climbed up to persuade the gunners not to fire on the protesters. I have a picture of that on my wall to remind me of what really matters.

That took guts. Or guys like the Special Forces soldier who threw himself on a grenade to save his buddies. Paddling doesn't rise to that. As influences, I'd say Walt Blackadar and Rob Lesser, and a friend of mine, Zap Erikson. In 1972 I was 14, and I had a subscription to *Sports Illustrated* and read Blackadar's story. That lit a fire. A couple years later I saw films of him getting utterly trashed on the Susitna (1975), which seemed awesome. That was about the time I learned how to roll and paddled a few times on our local runs. Then I dropped it. But Lesser on the Stikine defined the sport for me; at that point I became inspired to really start paddling (1981).

Zap was a friend of mine on the swim team in the early 1970s who learned how to roll, got bone cancer, and at 18 in 1973, paddled the upper part of the North Fork Payette in a fiberglass boat. He had one leg at the time. He skied, parachuted, climbed, and finally died from cancer in 1984, but he never stopped joking and he never complained, even after eight operations and the loss of both legs. Zap is a hero to me, but not because of his kayaking.

What sport led you to kayaking?
Although I liked kayaking, I did it only sporadically, and mostly not in terms of whitewater. Kayaking came after swimming, climbing, cliff jumping, backpacking, and skiing. However, it wasn't some other sport that led me into it, it was playing classical guitar. I paddled early on, but it wasn't until I'd been a fanatic classical guitarist for a number of years that I really appreciated rivers. I was looking for a different kind of music to play, and I found it in the current and flowing water. At that point, kayaking became my instrument of choice, and rivers my music of choice. It was the perfect synthesis of everything I liked – free flowing emotion, power, athleticism, challenge, problem-solving, beauty, outdoors – it just had everything and I charged into it in every way. I think the combination of swimming and guitar allowed me to understand the feeling of flow, which almost immediately defined my sense of the sport.

Classify your development as a kayaker: I got really good really fast, was paddling hard class V within one season after focusing on the sport. Hard knocks as well as lots and lots of training and doing everything I could to learn.

Ways and advice to advance: Okay grasshopper, here it is: Let otters be your inspiration. Learn to play with the water in all its moods and forms. Never fight it, never feel conflict. To paddle at the highest level you need to belong in each river you move with. Any nervousness shows your weakness, so find and remove every weakness. Train slalom, play paddle, run every kind of river, creek, pond, lake, and ocean you can touch, paddle every kind of boat, catch every eddy you can, surf every wave, do every move possible, learn everything about what the current does — you'll never succeed but trying is an awful lot of fun — feel the music of the water, apply skateboarding and music and martial arts to paddling and learn how to ricochet and ride and slide off of rock features. Paddle the way an otter would if he had a kayak. He doesn't need one, and you need to get to the place where it is part of you.

Classify your development. Does it come from being totally prepared?
You can never be totally prepared for a step into the unknown. Prepare the best you can, don't underestimate things, always be learning and developing.

Why were you drawn toward creeking? Over the years I've done 40+ first descents. I liked exploring and figuring things out – the water levels, logistics, where and when to go, how to get there. Translating what you could see on a map to what might be paddleable. It's totally different now with google earth and easily obtained satellite photos. We were the first people to start really hiking in around this region, in the mid-1980s. There was lots to do. Lots of promise, lots of great runs.

<u>What teaches your more: hard knocks?</u> Hard knocks.

<u>What helped you progress?</u> Always being focused on gaining new skills and improving the old. Constantly searching for how it all fit together. Never at rest. Always seeking deeper understanding.

<u>Who are your sponsors?</u> Before 1990 I paddled with Perception, but that was because they were essentially the only manufacturer around, and also because Rob Lesser was my close friend and made sure I could try out anything new that came along. There was no money involved, just the possibility of getting gear at a wholesale rate, or in some cases, Rob giving me gear after he had used it as demos for a season. The issue never really came up until Dagger started in the late 80s, and then in about 1993 when the company teams started. At that point, I rejected sponsorship. I had been invited to be on several company teams, which was flattering, but after I thought about it for a little bit I decided the answer had to be no. To me, kayaking is about independence, and I prefer to go my own way. Swag never appealed much to me, and I don't like wearing stickers. I went to the river because it was free of all that, and so deliberately bringing all the trappings of mainstream companies and ego there is the opposite of why I paddle. I can't imagine doing nothing but driving around and running rivers, competing at freestyle or Class V races. Some people may like it, but it sounds pretty boring to me. There's so much more to life than that. It's a trifling way to live, even if it's fun for a while.

I realize that sponsorship is a given for most excellent paddlers these days, and a few of them even expect sponsorship as if it's a rite of passage, an affirmation of their skills, or even an entitlement for "helping" the companies. They don't seem to realize that when you look at the cost-benefit from the company's standpoint, sponsored athletes aren't worth it. They are completely expendable. However, on a personal level I think sponsorship can also potentially become a kind of virus. My paddling means certain things to me because I have deliberately kept it outside of commercial concerns. I realized in the early 1990s, which also coincided with my focus on soloing, that I was seeking a certain kind of purity of experience. I was seeking something that rivers and kayaking couldn't give me if I had any other motives or influences, and so I pared away all formal ties to companies. That purity is what gives kayaking its value to me. That's not for everybody, but it is the opposite extreme from seeking sponsorship.

I think nearly all paddlers share this feeling of purity about their experiences; it's really the core of the river's draw. So, I believe all of us have this in common. I think I took it farther than most. While I don't question how strong their love for rivers and paddling is, I do think sponsorship changes how they think about what they do. A few years back there was a major uproar among manufacturers and competition promoters because some of the sponsored paddlers were so obnoxious. Clearly it went to their heads. Fortunately most are not like that. Some of this is inevitable because it mixes personal and social reward. There's so little money in the sport that the effects are relatively small. And the river experiences are so powerful they also tend to overwhelm any covetousness.

Among the sponsored athletes you have intelligent, highly talented young men and women who are experts at a fascinating sport, traveling the world dealing with both beautiful and dangerous surroundings. On the surface, that would seem like a crucible for some penetrating thoughts about life. Yet, where are they? As best I can tell, that lifestyle doesn't produce such thinking. Instead, it produces a kind of continuous excitement and intense fun that substitutes for thinking, as if the lifestyle is the answer to everything. These guys are great paddlers, but the sponsorship just feeds a self-referential way of being. Their films are their expression of life, but most are all action and no reflection, which is why it's called whitewater porn. People who are "paid to play" aren't the ones who will provide us with a philosophy to live by. The more sponsorship they get, the farther removed they are from the rest of us into a kind of fantasy land, and the less they have to offer outside of the action. Self-focused fun instead of perspective. It's fine for them, but it's never been something I aspired to. For me personally, I see it as the opposite of what I want my own kayaking to be. But the most important thing here is, nobody should impose his definitions. Certainly I don't want or intend that, so to each his own. Paddling is all about individual freedom.

Do you have any doubts and fears? How do you deal with them?
If you're doubtful or fearful, then don't paddle. If you're feeling those emotions, they are your inner self-being honest and mean you're over your head, either physically or mentally or both. If you're fearful then you're ruining your paddling and also just asking for an accident. Back off to easier rivers, train, improve your skills in every way possible, and most of all enjoy yourself. If you do this and work systematically on your skills and conditioning, then you'll know when you're ready for the next step because at some point it will seem like the perfect thing to do. You might be excited, but you won't be fearful and you won't doubt. Also, keep in mind, you don't have to do harder things. There's no rule out there that says you need to paddle Class V or even Class IV. Go out and have fun at whatever level you find enjoyable. If fear appears, look carefully at why, solve the issues that cause it, and ask yourself whether you're doing something you really want to do.

Fear is your honest self telling you what your limits are. Listen to it. I won't paddle with somebody who is fearful; I'll tell them to go do something easier, or I'll take them and we'll paddle someplace easier. I'll suggest they ask themselves why they want to be on a run that frightens them, because that's fodder for some psychotherapy. It indicates that they have extra unspoken reasons for being there, and those reasons are not in line with their own internal assessment of what they are capable of. They need to think about that, find a better match between river and self, or improve their skills so they know they are a good match for that run. The crux is, they're asking their paddling to take them someplace they don't belong. It might be something for ego — to feel they belong on the Green, North Fork Payette, Yule Creek, Upper Cherry, or some other notorious run, so they strive to be a 'member' of what they see as the elite. Sometimes it's driven by a sense of accomplishment, or of proving themselves — but none of those are necessarily good reasons for putting oneself in a life-threatening situation. If they start out doubting and fearful, then it is likely they will not be thinking clearly when the show is on, they will not be adequate team partners, and that is very likely to get them really scared, or hurt — or put their companions in danger as well. Be honest enough to accept fear, and be courageous enough to do something intelligent about it, instead of selfishly putting yourself and your teammates at risk. Bravado doesn't cut it either. It's just a half step from fear.

If you're constantly dealing with fears and doubts, then there's something seriously wrong with the way you are approaching the sport. Go out and do something easy and fun, Class III or easy Class IV at most. You should be getting satisfaction and joy out of the very act of paddling.

***

Section Three: Putting It All Together

The Real Measure of Skill

Author's note:

At the advice of several friends, below are portions of one letter I wrote to a paddler who attempted the Grand Canyon of the Stikine. This 60-mile section of the Stikine is one of the hardest expedition rivers in the world, coursing through a deep gorge in Northern British Columbia.

In the following, I changed the names to keep the two paddlers relatively anonymous. Because there are many people in the sport who want to try the hardest runs, some of the problems these guys had also have happened to other groups. Such runs involve life and death and have to be taken with great seriousness. The critical question that is hardest to answer is, "am I ready for this?" The excerpts below deal with some of the most important things that go into what makes for being ready. In the end, nobody can answer any of the big questions except the person himself, and sometimes he (or she) cannot know unless they try. You need to be realistic, and not reach so far beyond your skills that you get killed. The following offers some very pointed suggestions, with details about this specific, difficult expedition river. This is a run I know well, having been on it four times and doing three descents, including a solo run in 1992.

A sketch of the attempt:

One partner (Ralph) had attempted the Stikine canyon several years before, but had bailed off early (right below Entry Falls) when the weather suddenly turned cold and it snowed. He wanted to go back, but needed the right partner. He met Ben two seasons ago. They became friends and paddled a lot together on some difficult runs. Ben was an ambitious paddler, ready for bigger challenges. He also was married and had children. His wife was not a kayaker and was not happy to have him trying to do the Stikine. He and Ralph planned a year in advance for the run, but much of the preparation was scattered, and they didn't paddle as much as they had intended. They felt reasonably confident and decided to go for it anyway. They chartered a chopper, and flew the narrow canyon looking at the run from about 40 feet up. After the levels see-sawed they had a window with a plausible level, and put on. One other team had just paddled the run.

From the first major rapid (Entry Falls), Ben was distracted, worried about his wife and his preparation. He was not concentrating well and felt unsteady in his heavily loaded boat. He was using an unfamiliar bent-shaft paddle, with gloves, and had difficulties with his braces and roll, having to make many attempts and feeling somewhat out of control in the big rapid and its run out. He quickly began feeling fatigued, and his hands started cramping. They ran Entry and 3 Goat rapid, several other unnamed rapids, portaged Wicked Wanda, and then camped. Ralph had fallen during the portage and hurt his shoulder pretty badly, probably tearing his rotator cuff. They ran one more rapid the next morning, then decided to break off the attempt given that Ralph was hurt and Ben was not feeling solid enough. So they climbed out at Pass-Fail, on river right. They intended to hike down to Site Zed along the rim, then put back on.

Instead they got lost, overshot and spent another night out up on the rim, now downstream of Site Zed. Then they tried to get back to the river by following a side stream down to the water. It got much too steep and they backed out, climbing up a side ridge and realizing they were lost. They spent several days there, trying to make smoke as a fixed wing plane and several helicopters went by and didn't spot them. They had not made it out on time, and had been reported missing by Ben's wife. On the fourth day, they were seen and the chopper pilot was able to do a precarious skid landing and get them out.

The letter contains excerpts of my candid responses. I didn't send it at first, but finally I felt that honesty and reality required I tell Ben what I thought, since he had made contact with me first and had sent a long written account. I don't like being critical, but when we are dealing with life and death issues, and when people are ambivalent and making mistakes that can get them killed, you need to say it like you see it. I've omitted a great deal, choosing only those comments with general application to all of us.

Here are some of the questions addressed:

"What is the real measure of skill?"

"When are you ready to take on a river like this?"

"How do you prepare and approach difficult runs?"

"What equipment do you decide to bring?"

"How do you make sure your roll is good enough?"

Dear Ben:

I've read your account twice and have a few comments. I know it is difficult to put down thoughts and feelings on paper, so I understand the struggle and don't want the comments below to sound overly critical. They aren't intended that way. It's more of a post mortem or autopsy to see what we can learn so we do better the next time.

I'm almost positive that the rapid you called Wicked Wanda is actually an unnamed rapid above Three Goat. The canyon widens some after Entry, goes through some Class IV, a side stream comes in (Leatham Creek), and then the walls start rising and the canyon starts closing in. It's probably about a mile to a mile and a half below Entry. As the walls get vertical and maybe 200 feet high, the next big rapid is Three Goat, which is basically one major drop with some large diagonals and then the main current right of center drops into a very large hole and turbulent runout. At lower water there are two river-wide ledge holes. I believe the rapid you call Three Goat is actually Wicked Wanda – the one with the large boulder down at the bottom on river left (normally a huge exploding wave). After the real Three Goat, the canyon narrows and there are some rapids, but nothing big. The canyon opens up right as you get to Wicked Wanda, which apparently you portaged. Looking upstream from it you see vertical black walls, but at the rapid and downstream the canyon walls move back a bit from the water, on river left there is a broad, open and loose boulder slope going up into a near vertical, light colored, highly stratified sedimentary rock cliff that is probably 600-700 feet above the river. Downstream around a bend, and across a 200-300 yard slower stretch, the black bedrock comes out again and there is an unnamed rapid in a quick S-turn (which is probably about where you camped on the river left ledge, and the rapid you ran first the second day), then you move into the lead-in to Pass-Fail as the walls close in. At Pass Fail they are notched in, vertical for about 50 to 100 feet, then open up some above, making it hard but possible to climb out. Downstream from there, they just keep getting higher and vertical straight out of the water. Around the corner at the bottom of Pass Fail is another small rapid and then you go directly into Wasson's and what we call the upper Narrows.

You describe getting cramps in your hands and arms, being overheated and struggling with your loaded boat in the big rapids. You also mention feeling sluggish, barely able to roll, and losing your confidence.

In addition to what you diagnose about the reasons you were cramping (using gloves and a different paddle), it also means you were not in good enough physical condition, and that you were way too anxious and clutching the paddle with a death grip. The only times I've ever seen paddlers get cramps like that is when they were over their heads and really anxious, gripping the paddle about five times as hard as they needed to be. Your grip on the paddle should only be just enough to hold it and make it do what you need. Any harder or any lighter is a mistake. The samurai described the proper grip for holding their swords was "like holding a bird" – just firm enough to keep it from getting away, but not hard enough to hurt the bird. The same is true for paddles.

I think this problem also speaks volumes about whether you really were prepared at a gut level – both mentally and physically – for doing the river. I think it shows you weren't. You changed gear, used a paddle you were less secure with, in a loaded boat you weren't comfortable with, struggling for control, and were anxious and tense. Don't take that badly, the object here is to understand what happened so you don't repeat the errors...

***

Here is a reality check. You need to do some major recalibration. At your camp below Wicked Wanda, in terms of whitewater you were approximately $1/10^{th}$ of the way through the canyon, and hadn't paddled any of the hardest rapids. You were three named rapids out of about 25 into the canyon, and you portaged one of them (Wicked Wanda). The other rapids you describe are unnamed and minor in comparison – even if they are big – and there are probably another 60 such rapids through the canyon. In fact, by the third day, people are absolutely amazed at how much incredible whitewater there is. Realistically, you were just nibbling on the beginning of the canyon. You were too slow and too hesitant – meaning that the skill level required is one where you're looking at those rapids and seeing quickly what you need to do and not having any doubts about whether you can do it. I debated whether I should write this next sentence, but frankly, if you portaged Wicked Wanda, then you probably shouldn't be trying to do the canyon. There are at least 15 rapids that are harder by a considerable amount and many of them do not have easy portaging like WW – and believe me, even if you felt it was hard, actually that is easy portaging compared to elsewhere. Please understand I'm just trying to state things realistically here. It's a very good thing you got out at Pass-Fail because if you'd portaged, put in at the bottom of it and gone around the corner, you would have really been upset confronting Wasson's. Wasson's is committing, bizarre, and damnedly intimidating even when one is paddling well and hasn't had any trouble to that point. In addition to Wasson's there are many other rapids downstream that are much more intimidating and difficult than anything you saw. These are, in particular, the Wall and then the final set of six or eight rapids in the lower Narrows. I think it was an extremely good decision that you stopped when you did and got out safely.

You have to have a better sense of place, the canyon and wilderness around the river. The rapids are not the only thing you have to deal with if you have to bail off the run. Almost every team that has climbed out has gotten lost up on the rim because it is really hard to tell where you are. When you flew the canyon, I'm certain your eyes were on the water and rapids, but they are only part of the issue – the rest is the canyon walls, which determine where you can get in and out, and the weird rolling plateau and forest above on the rim. You won't see any of that stuff if you are only focused on the river. But once off the river, they are critical.

You said you were 40 feet off the water, which means that you couldn't gain an appreciation for the terrain along the canyon rim below Zed, because it's all 500 to 1000 feet straight over your head. So when you were out of the canyon, once you realized you were below Zed you couldn't know how ill-advised it was to head back toward the river from any point along there. I don't understand your decision. I don't know why you couldn't tell from the topo map that there were cliffs and huge problems in getting back to the river. Even the large scale Canadian Geological Survey maps with 40 meter contours show this. Reaching the river is either extremely difficult for the first few miles, or impossible after that without full-on difficult climbing and rappelling for many hundreds of feet, or even 1000+ feet a few miles farther. Didn't that show up on your map? Did you have a topo map? Site Zed is one of the very few places where there is a reasonable route to and from the river, but on either side of it, both upstream and downstream, are huge bluffs fully 800 to 1000 feet straight up out of the water. It's horrendous. Below it a few miles is the second major narrow section which extends for much of the next 10 miles. My eyes widened when I read you tried to follow a stream back down to the river. That sounds crazy to me. The only place I know of where one can get back to the river in a semi reasonable way is clear down past the second narrows, below the rapid called "The Wall", at the "Garden of the Gods." There must be others, but that's at least ten to twelve miles downstream. And it isn't easy there either, as there are huge sandstone cliffs with intermittent gullies, boulder slopes, and loose, steep scree. A friend of mine from Smithers studied the goats in there for years and said that when it rained, refrigerator, car, and house sized boulders were coming down regularly. He said it was a terrifying place to work. And I would expect it to take two or three days of bushwacking to get there from where you were.

Also, every single creek in there creates its own major canyon, and goes off repeated 50 to 200 foot falls before it gets back to the river. Creekbeds are always slippery, lack holds, are very awkward even when they aren't dropping off the face of the earth. It's fortunate that you didn't go any farther down that creek, or you would have been cliffed out without being able to backtrack. And why were you doing it in twilight? One slip in the wrong place and either you or Ralph would have been gone. Nobody would have found you if you'd been trapped in some little side canyon like that away from the river. I have to be honest and say that was not a good decision. I also have to say that the sequence of decisions was questionable – going downstream from Pass-Fail instead of back upstream toward the bridge, to overshooting Zed, to heading back toward the river along a creek, not knowing what was there. I don't understand any of that and it most certainly is not what I would do. The two good decisions were deciding to bail off the run at Pass Fail, and getting out of the creek bed and up onto the ridge. I also know that things which seem reasonable at the time because of how one is thinking sometimes look very different later on. So I don't want to sound overly critical. However, we are talking about living and dying here.

It's not my place to tell people what they should and shouldn't do, but I feel I need to be bluntly honest: if you have to portage Wicked Wanda and Pass Fail, it means you need to rethink whether you're up to the run. Those are difficult rapids, but if you didn't look at them and say with confidence "That's hard, but I can do it", then the canyon probably isn't the place you should be – yet. I think you are overreaching right now, and there is too wide a gap between your desire and your skills. If you intend to try it again, you should consider working *very* hard for at two or more seasons to get appreciably more skilled in big water, in better shape, with more experience, and more confidence running big water Class V in a loaded boat. I'm not talking about normal years of boating. That isn't enough. I'm talking about kicking it up five notches from where you are and peaking for this river.

Here's the real measure of skill, or at least, how I measure it. It doesn't matter what you can paddle in optimum circumstances. It doesn't matter what you can paddle when you are rested, feeling good, confident, with an unloaded boat. What matters is that you can paddle big water Class V+ even when you're exhausted, feeling lousy, hurt, and your confidence is shot. The problem with your whole approach is that you're looking at what you can do in the best of circumstances. Competent expeditioning demands something totally different – what you can do when the worst happens and you're at rock bottom. That is the level you should be judging. You should still be able to paddle at the highest level the river requires even when everything is going wrong. That's the only measure of skill that matters here.

You mention the book *Into Thin Air*. That's actually an exaggeration of the present problems and a great case study in futility and bad judgment. All the people who died in the fiasco on Mount Everest recounted by Krakauer were more or less fine as long as the weather was good, the guides could help them, the trail was set, they were attached to the fixed lines, the fixed lines were in good shape, the ascenders weren't icing up, the oxygen tanks were working great, and there were no problems. Half of them died when there was a storm – because they didn't have the skills to climb Everest or even escape from it when things started going wrong. It was a completely predictable example of a people who didn't belong up there. The last 20 years of guiding on Everest have shown that somebody who goes with a guide, has decent skills, has good luck with weather and conditions, is in excellent shape and acclimatizes well can potentially climb Everest – at least in the best of circumstances. That's actually amazing. But there is a problem that comes up and the *Thin Air* fiasco illustrates it perfectly. If something happens, they aren't lucky, and the outcome suddenly relies on their judgment and skill, then you have a different situation. A person slips and the other guy on the rope has to react to arrest the fall; or they have to arrest their own. The weather goes bad. They have to navigate in a whiteout, or after their oxygen is gone. They get hurt and have to deal with it and get themselves off the mountain. Anybody less than a deep expert will likely die if suddenly exposed to less than the best of circumstances. And if things are bad enough, the experts will die too, as witness the two main guides who died there during that trip, and the 11 excellent climbers who just died on K2.

The entire situation was avoidable. *Into Thin Air* is a centerpiece for how not to climb or do any adventure sport – and how hubris and cavalier attitudes (or even just incomplete judgment) and the core issues we're talking about here come into play. None of us would want somebody like Krakauer writing our story after we died in the Stikine, slamming us, calling into question every one of our decisions, interviewing our families and friends and painting a picture of somebody overreaching. None of us would want to look like that doctor who was on his third expedition and ended up nearly dying, losing his ears and nose to frostbite, miraculously surviving, and apologizing to his family for making them pay for his self-centered obsession.

You want to have a great experience and live to come home and talk about it. Given that, you have to measure preparation and competence differently. You have to ask, "Do I belong here?" and realistically answer "yes." Measure competence by what you can do when everything goes wrong and all the things you planned are screwed – and yet you still have the skill and endurance to deal with it all. That is the real measure - not what you can do when everything is going right and all your plans are working. So we know you can't run the Stikine when you're feeling unconfident, unsteady, your arms are cramping, you're tired, distracted, feeling guilty about your wife and kids, and your partner is hurt. Now the question is, if you want to go back, how are you going to change things so you have a reasonable chance of success?

However, a bigger question that I asked in the earlier email is, why do you even want to do it? And don't answer that to me, because the only answer that matters is to yourself, your wife, your children, and those who love you.

And despite all the considerations above, it is also true that people can rise to the occasion, and so I always keep open that possibility. But it didn't work out this time, and it's not something to rely on.

Consider the aspect of paddling with fatigue or injuries. Last time through the canyon I broke two ribs in the first rapid below Entry (before Three Goat). It's a no-name rapid (the one you thought was Three Goat) but it clobbered me, I was in an awkward twisted position, caught by a surge from a breaking wave and – kaboom – my side exploded. I was in excruciating pain and could hardly roll. Once up in the eddy below, I confided to Charlie Munsey that I had a serious injury. Then I gritted my teeth, shut up, and paddled. From almost any standpoint, that was probably very, very stupid, but I decided to do it and I did it. I nailed my lines in everything. To me, the Stikine means that if you go in, you'd better be able to come out the other end. Please note that even with two broken ribs I was still able to paddle everything, and even did one difficult drop that neither Rob Lesser, Charlie Munsey, Gerry Moffatt or the others would do.

I don't advise this, and it may all be very stupid from any normal person's standpoint, but it shows the skill level I'm talking about. I know I can still paddle the hardest Class V+ for three days, in the rain, when I'm beat, and even when I have two broken ribs. If you can't, then you should question whether you have the skills to be there. I can do and have done rapids at least two or three grades harder when things are going great, but I never count on things going great on an expedition because I've learned you simply cannot expect it. If it happens, then good, but expect less and even consider the opposite. I've done dozens of trips where injuries, sickness, fatigue, distractions from team arguments, personality conflicts, and a hundred other things were present, and I know I can paddle the hardest rapids that can be done, and do it well, for days and weeks, even when all that shit is going wrong. *You should measure your skill level by what your poorest paddling is.* If that skill level is up to the Stikine, then you have a good chance of doing it safely. Never assume you can sketch through stuff and things will come out okay, because that attitude will get you killed. It's easy enough to get killed even when we're doing well, but when we start sketching, then our worst paddling better be up to the job or we're asking for it.

***

The (apparent) problems you guys had were serious. However, you both survived, so it's clear you handled what you needed to. This should be treated as a huge learning experience, and the choices need to be better. Note if just one additional thing had happened, the ending could easily have been very bad.

However, every with all the comments above, I have to admit that in 1989, my partner Bob McDougall got obliterated and we could have had a total disaster too. It's even possible that all three of us (Bob, Rob Lesser, and me) could have died in one lousy undercut hole in Entry Falls, so I'm not going to say it can't happen to the rest of us because it obviously can. Gerry Moffatt got wedged under a boulder, John Wasson, Lars Holbeck, Fred Coriell, and John Grace swam in pretty desperate situations. Nobody had a sure thing in there. That's why we have to have all the pieces in place and the highest level of skill possible. Even with that, any of us could be killed.

I think the track record shows Ralph has been cautious, working within his skill level. On his earlier attempt and this one, he got out when he was too stretched. That was prudent and cautious. However, the big problem in my mind – and I would ask you to put it in capitals – is this: *the main canyon and main drops CANNOT be done by being cautious. The Stikine is a run that will never yield to caution.* You won't have the luxury of getting out when you're feeling stretched. You'll be trapped and the only way out is downstream through a "must run" rapid. You have to be damn good, and willing and capable of working through the place no matter what. If somebody doesn't have the skill and confidence to do that, then they shouldn't go in.

There's always a "but": so, beyond all these considerations, we have to acknowledge it is possible to run it without being one of the best paddlers in the world, and you can look through the list of people who have been there and see that. However, never underestimate people! From what I've seen, people can and do rise to the occasion, and paddle better than they ever have before, so be careful: don't just pick a name and say "if he can do it, then I can too." It also depends on who their partners are and what their partners bring out of them. You can never tell what that will be. The balance in all this comes also from not underestimating yourself. You have abilities and depth you haven't reached; it's true for all of us. I know taken together all this sounds almost self-contradictory, or at least paradoxical, but if it were easy and straightforward, we wouldn't be doing this sport and we wouldn't be drawn to these places.

***

You mention a team before you. You need to be careful of another kind of false reasoning: assuming that just because one group did it, another group can do it too. It depends (at least) on how the teams compare to each other. Further, knowing it's possible doesn't mean that you – or I – will also be able to do it. The group was A and a friend of his (M from Quebec). I don't know M, but I do know A. Even if only in his early 20s you have to realize that he is a very, very good paddler, with huge motivation and a very sharp focus on the Stikine. He had been there twice before, neither was a good experience. He got stuffed badl-

y once in Wasson's with the LVM crew in 2005, nearly drowned, and hiked out from Zed, so he knew what he would have to
deal with in there. He didn't put on the second time due to high
water, after hiking into Entry Falls to scout. So when he came
back this year for the third time, he was in an aggressive and
focused mode mentally, just itching to prove he could do it, and
he was super prepared and strong. He had been corresponding
with me for the year-and-a-half prior, asking for advice, had
paddled 300+ days the preceding year, and trained like a maniac
that entire time. He'd done multiple hard runs in the preceding
months, and was in great paddling condition mentally and physically. He was already an excellent paddler, and he made sure he
was peaking for the Stikine.

If you look at that comparison to your situation you'll
see that it was not wise to think that if his team could do it, you
could too. You had about one-fifth or even one-tenth the
preparation he did, both mentally and physically. So to do it the
same way he did, you'd have to be five to ten times as good a
paddler – which is not possible. He's a solid member of the excellent younger guys in the sport. By his own admission he has
some weaknesses in his technique, and can improve, but he also
has the huge life force of youth, complete motivation, no family
responsibilities or distractions, and has been paddling very widely year round. The final straw is, he was honed and strong mentally while you were ambivalent and distracted.

A few other points: It sounds like your boat was too
heavy. You should be able to handle your boat even when loaded. A loaded boat shouldn't weight more than about 70 pounds,
which is its base weight plus maybe 25 pounds of gear. Heavier
than that and you just can't portage it, and you certainly can't
paddle it well. It's a give that you'll have to portage in the Stikine – at a minimum Site Zed no matter how aggressive you are,
which is a taxing, dangerous, and precarious portage. And more
likely it will be five or six portages. I did six on our 1990 descent, two on my solo, and three in 1998. Because V-Drive has
changed, it now can be done with one. The point is, doing any

more than that is an ordeal, so you better be able to move your boat around without undue difficulty. It might make fine sense to have a heavier boat if you're on a long river trip that doesn't require high end technical paddling and portaging, but that's not the Stikine.

***

You should never change equipment before a trip. Use only the things you have been paddling with. Certainly never change something as vital as a paddle. This is a major mistake...

If you were having trouble rolling, then regardless of the gear, the paddle, the boat, or anything else, your roll isn't good enough. Go and do another 5000 rolls on each side, carefully working your technique until getting up is almost effortless, and then put some rocks in the boat and fill it half full with water and do another 5000 on each side with the same attention to technique. Then talk to me about whether your present roll was good enough. I wouldn't suggest it if I hadn't already done it myself.

Again, just like with paddling hard whitewater, your roll is measured by how good it is when everything goes wrong. If with a loaded boat, a new offset paddle, turbulent whitewater, an injured shoulder, cramping hands, you can't get up immediately with little effort, then I rest my case – by Stikine standards, it isn't good enough. I speak from direct experience, as my ability to roll has saved my life at least twice after major injuries in the middle of Class V+/VI whitewater. One of those times I hit a boulder full-on going about 30 mph, got plastered on the sharp leading edge. I was almost knocked out, it dislocated my collarbone, ripped virtually every shred of cartilage in my sternum, separated my shoulder, tore the muscles in my neck and down my back, and nearly paralyzed me with pain. I couldn't move my right side, but I rolled up, got plunged badly, working out of huge holes for another 300 yards of nasty rapids, and finally made an eddy. I couldn't sleep for months afterward, and it took over a year to recover good function. That was 13 years ago and my shoulder still hurts, so that's a measure of how serious the injury was. But I rolled and I made it to an eddy in Class VI whitewater. If I hadn't, I'd be dead. That's my measure of whether a roll is good enough. If yours isn't up to that, then you'd better keep working on it.

Actually, that's a lie. It isn't my real measure of a good roll. My real measure is that I have always assumed my roll is never good enough, and I believe that to this day. Having that as my standard has allowed me to weather situations that should have killed me. Even knowing that, I will never stop working on and training my roll to make it even better. It is never good enough.

I'm not saying anything here that I haven't scoured myself with.

I hope these comments clarify the gap between what you are trying to do, and what you can do.

Good luck.

***

Coyote Falls

In his guidebook to Idaho whitewater, my good friend Grant Amaral calls running Coyote Falls on the South Fork of the Clearwater river, "a stunt at best", advisably only done at low-medium flows, such as 1500 cubic feet per second. That might be true, but is a testament to how differently we can see things. After getting acquainted with the run in the mid- to late 1980s, for six or seven years I headed over every time the water got high to run Coyote Falls and Golden Canyon, usually by myself. I can't claim that paddling alone is necessarily a great idea, but it doesn't deserve the taboo that is commonly nailed on it. You take the same precautions and you don't trust that God or the River will give you a pass if you make a mistake. You can run through your mind counting the friends who aren't around anymore, but there's no point in being paranoid or you'll stop paddling. It's a balance between faith in yourself and giving the river the respect it deserves, aware it might have other things up its sleeve.

I loved putting on and running Golden Canyon, especially at high water from 3000 to 5000cfs, or two to more than three times the flows Grant considered prudent. The road is almost empty, with no more than a car every 15 or 20 minutes near the end of the day. The early summer evenings are long, with the light reflected off the canyonsides, and the depth of the canyon holds the glow of the sun until it dims to dusk.

Coyote Falls is not really a waterfall, but a huge cascade rated class V at 1500cfs and lower on the Stites gauge. Grant says the few people who have done it have been very particular about the level, but that's only because I never told him about all the times I've run it at much higher flows. And if running it at 1500 is a stunt, then I don't know what it would be called from 3000 to over 5000, which were the levels I looked for. A dozen or so times I drove over Lolo pass and down the Lochsa, past all those great surf waves, past the Selway and up the South Fork to solo Golden Canyon and Coyote Falls.

At 3000cfs Coyote Falls is impressive, but at 5000 and above, the river is a sight to behold. The narrow canyon focuses the water in a sluice ricocheting through the truck sized boulders, crashing down through huge drops and massive holes, cloaked by a shower of misting spray. It is solid class VI+ with another quarter mile of class V+ below. Looking down at the manic water draws a primal urge out of you. It's a sense of freedom and energy, of purpose and possibilities, of life and the direct line to truth.

More than anything else, any paddler who has the balls to get up there and shove off has got to have his mental game under control. He's got to have absolute faith in his abilities and line. While scouting, the air reverberates with the sheer energy and roar, and you try to imagine yourself out in that chaos. It's hard to get the right frame of mind. Outwardly, you might find yourself thinking about a sled slamming through a minefield and shooting off a cliff. Or, of riding the back of an exploding stampede of water buffalo ripping through the forest, tearing trees up as they careen downhill. Up on the bank, the noise and roar hit you like something solid and you have to shout to be heard. And you can scout and shout all you want, standing up there on the bank pointing at things, closing your eyes and figuring angles. But the final question is always simple - are you going to run it?

The line is to the right because below 4000 the boulders still show in the middle, but around 5000 they form huge holes as the current bucks over them while its bulk shoots into the bank and is heaved roughly back into the center of the river, buckling into sharp ridges and diagonals of cresting water. The water no longer acts like it does in a normal river. It is so fast that the waves and holes spin sidewise, like pencil sharpeners twisting downstream instead of at right angles to the current. As the level gets higher, everything just gets louder and faster, more frenetic and violent.

Putting on above, it comes fast and furious. You run a big ledge hole at the first corner and flash through a short straightaway. You hear no noise at all; the roar and crashing are gone. There's only motion and power welling up beneath you, your eyes focused and staring at the horizonline with a feeling that the entire world is on the brink of some cataclysmic event. There's a brief surreal sense, as if the rapid below in the mist is not really there, but instead is someplace far away on the other side of the universe. For a moment you see the spray and the ragged tops of the waves as the water accelerates you toward the edge, and in that fleeting instant as you crest the first horizonline, you look down into the gut of the rapid. The earth itself suddenly gapes open in your path and breathes its full power. It is only that single, surreal instant but it lasts a million years, and then you're in the heart of it, the secret of life erupting around you in a supernova of spray.

Up and over the first huge diagonal waves, cresting and shooting down, keeping angle through another rebounding wave off the bank looming over you – a shuddering liquid animal that seethes and wants to drive you left into disaster, then a set of two ramping pencil sharpeners convulsing to keep the flow as they will it, spinning the world, and through another massive explode-ing wave hole, angling again on faith and your scout, flying straight into the crux drop, ricocheting to the left with the second truck sized hole so close you can touch it, and then into the class V+ runout.

Faith is really the word: faith in yourself, faith in your line and your ability to stay on it. An awareness that there is a higher power, but you are a following a small light leading through the madness and into the serenity beyond.

Somebody who doesn't understand the river might think that running a rapid like this would be all about muscle and fighting the water, but it's not. It's the most natural thing in the world to tense up at the thought of grappling with a raging river, fighting it and pitting strength against strength, but the truth is just the opposite. The more powerful the river is, the calmer you have to be. Your body must be drained of every bit of tension, leaving composure, even quietness in the midst of the exploding insanity.

There's a line there, a precise thread through the chaos, but frantic paddlestrokes won't let you touch it or ride it. Your calm and your tuned reflexes are what allow you to see it and enter it, joining with the power of the earth unleashed, a billion tons of snow released from winter's tight icy grasp and set free down the riverbed.

Some people even believe that whitewater is all about thrills, a hot and heavy battle with adrenaline, but they are wrong too. Outwardly it seems all power and violence, but it really has nothing to do with running with the bulls, shouting and excited and fearful with a thousand other people as the hooves and angry snorts of a dozen slavering animals pound the cobblestones at your heels. It's a different universe altogether. You can't jump aside into a doorway and let the bulls pass by. The river is none of those things. No, it is about the coolness of the matador in the face of a ceaseless herd of bulls who pour down the rough river-bed and never stop, who can't see you and don't respond to your cape. It's all about touching the wildness of the river, the ragged sheer energy while maintaining your sense of self. Every explosion has to be absorbed through the boat into your motion, and you fly through the air, balanced within and carried along by deep powers that sculpt the earth itself, threading a delicate line between life - and whatever is on the other side. In a sense, it is a measure of what makes us human – not behaving like an animal driven by fright, but looking straight at the threat of death and yet seeing clearly the beauty of life, shining like a star out of the darkness.

The long runout continues far around the next bend to the left, and is still hard class V+, but after the size and violence of Coyote Falls, somehow it seems easy. The river pushes on, interweaves into other rapids and fast running stretches all the way to the bottom of the canyon. There, if you're a little lucky and it's not too late, you can get a ride with your thumb. People are neighborly, and if they see you along the highway they are curious and friendly. It's not like Highway 55 along the North Fork Payette, where a constant stream of traffic and thousands of cars allow people to turn their heads away, and everybody thinks that some other driver will pick up the guy with the strange helmet, a life jacket and his thumb out, and they don't notice the look in his eye or that he's bleeding from his knuckles - the only evidence that some part of him touched the heart of the wild beast snorting and ripping apart the earth just off the safety of the bank.

One evening after I ran all the bigger rapids, in the middle stretch I came down on another of the many class IV rapids there. After running the wildness above, I eddied out to take a breather for a minute or so and enjoy the feel of having done one of the great rapids in the world and everything below on the fly - the feeling of unshakable faith in my line. A few breaths and a gaze at the late evening sky above, I glanced over my shoulder again, and ferried out of the eddy into the center of the river, skirting the edge of a set of holes on the top left, and turning with the current. Relaxed and smiling, I punched through a small hole and into a dark green wave.

My bow hit hard, and skittered upward, then the bottom of the boat slammed hard and the bow rocketed skyward as the back end settled down into the wave with a strange sinking feeling, as if being sucked under water. Suddenly I was looking up into the evening sky and thinking, *"What the hell...?:"*

The lights went out. The boat flipped backwards and shoved deep underwater, jammed upside down between the bottom and the submerged log I hadn't known was there.

Disoriented, my brain groped for order, struggling to get its bearings. The whole universe was scrambled and wrong. Somehow, I was upsidedown and backwards in the drop, deep deep underwater, and my brain was saying, *pry backwards, move back*, with knees unlocking and pushing to free me, my toes slipped off the footbrace, and the water bore down on me, flexing and bending the boat harder and harder against my knees and thighs.

Jets of water shoved up my nose, crammed up under my eyelids, and I felt the bites and stings of sand grains scoring my face, the huge hand of the river pressing me tight into the slot deep underwater, pinning the boat and me between the bottom and the log. In the murky water, I could faintly see my hands, the yellow boat, and the dark outline of the log against the sky.

The water tried to tear the paddle out of my hands. I forced my body backwards to minimize the pressure and feathered the paddle, the water caught it and nearly wrenched it from my grip again, slamming it down against the bottom, I feathered it slightly the other way and the water caught it again and slammed upward into the log.

I bucked backwards, bucked again, pushing with the paddle against the log, prying to loosen my body from the water's grip. A massive surge, I could feel the boat flexing and bending again, trapping my legs. Water crammed up under my eyelids as if it was going to pluck them right out of my head, and I felt the neck of my dry top bulge as it filled with water like a parachute, the current catching the top of my life jacket straining to rip it off, dragging harder and harder. My paddle blade cut into the log, my arms were tiring and a voice in the back of my mind calmly said, "*you're running out of air*". Another surge, another, and another - and suddenly I was wrenched free and all the pressure was released, washing downstream and rag-dolling underwater, tumbling with the current through another hole.

Breaking the surface I snatched a breath of air, my paddle still in my clenched hands. I spear-chucked it toward shore so I could swim, then body-slammed into a boulder, taking it right in the ribs, momentarily cartwheeled into a hole, helmet scraping against the bottom, then driving to the surface for another gulp of air and swimming again for the bank before the next rapid. Reaching the side, I belly crawled onto a boulder, breathing hard. A quick squeegee of the water out from under my eyelids, then I scrambled up the bank and set off running down the road to keep an eye on my boat.

A quarter mile or so, it swept into a log jam, I climbed down and grabbed the end, peeled it off the logs and pulled it into an eddy to dump the water out, finally lifting it into the rip-rapped boulders on the bank below the road.

There for the first time I stopped, sitting on my upside-down boat, breathing deep, checking all the pieces of me and my gear. *Jesus*. Everything accounted for.

I walked slowly back up the highway, breathing hard from the struggle underwater, the bruised ribs, the swim and racing down the road. My mind was a jumble. I picked up my paddle from where I'd thrown it into the rocks, and after a few more minutes of walking, reached the rapid.

At first I questioned whether it was the right one. There were the holes at the top, the wave in the middle, the holes below, the lead-in to the next rapid. *This has to be it, but what did I hang up on?* I couldn't see anything. From up on the road, it was a middling class IV rapid and nothing special, one move threading several holes, down into the big green wave in the center, right where I'd gone, then angling right through the bottom holes. *What happened?* I scanned the rapid again and again, up and down, and felt puzzled. Was this really the right rapid? Then I looked at the far bank in the rocks, and I saw it.

The log was about a foot in diameter. Its splintered end stuck out of the water just a few inches between two boulders on the bank, dark and nearly black, and angled directly out into the rapid almost perpendicular to the current, gradually going deeper and deeper into the center of the river. It must have hung up here at lower water. When the runoff rose, it got buried by the water and caught crosswise against the boulders by the pressure from the current instead of washing free. Out in the center, right in the line I'd run, it was at least four feet underwater and hidden in the base of the dark green wave that it helped make. The same wave I'd tried to punch and that had punched me back.

I looked for a few minutes more and the thoughts kept coming, sober and clear. How would I ever have seen it? This is just like any of the other class IVs on the run, all boat scoutable and two grades easier than Coyote Falls and below. I would never have gotten out to scout this rapid – and even if I had, I would not have seen the log. It was totally hidden. If I'd been in a smaller boat, my bow would have gone under and I'd have had the log in my lap, or shoved under facing forward and trapped in the boat. It's possible the front of the boat would have wrapped around the log and broken my legs. In any case, I probably would have drowned because nobody would have been able to help me. Even if I hadn't been solo, or even if there had been anybody on the road, there was no way for them to do anything. I had been pinned upsidedown, far underwater in fast moving current, with no way to anchor a safety line, and no way to reach me.

As the truth of the situation sank in, I realized I'd been holding my breath while the possibilities played through my head. I let out a long slow whistle and silently thanked the river for another chance at this thing we call life.

Even after that little experience on the South Fork of the Clearwater, I'm not a fatalist, but it's hard not to think that sooner or later a river may demand its due. Regardless of how experienced you are, that will come in a place of its choosing, at a time and for reasons you have no way to know or predict. Not in the most dramatic or hardest rapids, but in something that looks easy, because in addition to its beauty, the water sometimes hides its cards until you've played your hand. That's part of its wonder and the illusion of our control. The flip side is that you can die in a simple rapid and nobody will ever know why.

I don't paddle hard whitewater because I have a death wish or love thrills. I paddle because it is one of the most beautiful experiences I've ever found in 40 years of searching for truth on this planet. However, I now define a line as the route that takes you through the rapid - and into the rest of your life. It isn't true that disaster lurks in every wave. Our faith in ourselves creates infinite possibilities, yet in the river there is only one reality. Our lives depend on telling the difference in the instant when it matters most. When all is said and done, God may look after children and fools, but for the rest of us, a little paranoia might be a very good thing.

***

Zanshin

People differ greatly in how they approach running rapids. The mindset for how you engage harder whitewater develops over a long period of time. It changes as you progress, ebbing with setbacks and flowing forward with success. It is also built deeply on your training and practice, and sheer time on the water making decisions and moves. Beginners and intermediates often ask questions about how to approach rivers that are hard for them, and they receive thousands of suggestions for how they should do it.

Those who never have an accident – be it for skill or luck – typically have a nice simple feeling of excitement and anticipation. The combination of their natural abilities and the Grace of God gives their minds a confident feeling that everything will be fine; some even become cavalier and seem disrespectful. Others have a harder time of it, and confront demons of different sorts. Those demons might be the result of an accident or a bad experience, or perhaps a friend or instructor who burned into their mind the image of some impending disaster – a horrific broach or being trapped underwater – that they can't shake and whose specter seems to hide around every bend. Most people are somewhere in between – feeling the fun but also a bit uneasy and lacking confidence as they reach higher levels of difficulty.

Among the suggestions I've heard for dealing with harder whitewater, and especially Class V, are comments like, "If you're not nervous you shouldn't be here." Or, "You should be as nervous as when you first started." I agree with the intent of these statements, which is to remind you that running harder rapids can put you in situations where it is possible to be injured or killed. They underscore the idea that you should respect the river, not be overconfident, and take the situation seriously. However, I totally disagree with what these statements actually say. I don't think they capture the right frame of mind, and that's because the people saying them don't have the right concepts.

They know what they mean, but they don't have the words to say it very well.

The problem is that nervousness isn't respect, it is fear. Think about what "nervousness" means. Its synonyms are "anxious", "tense", "edgy", and "uneasy." If you're truly anxious about running a river, or tense and uneasy, then I'd suggest that you shouldn't put on. Don't make a habit of running things that scare you; that's overreaching and bad judgment. Other than exceptional circumstances such as an exploratory expedition or a carefully chosen next step in personal challenge, it is probably foolish to pursue your recreation into the realm of serious nerves and anxiety.

In general, feeling nervous should be taken as an intuitive prod that you are about to try something you really shouldn't be doing. Listen to that inner voice. But if it's not nervousness that we should feel, then what is the mindset one needs to run a river in balance, with confidence, respect, and with the proper sense of care no matter how challenging it is?

About 20 years ago I came across a word from the martial arts that perfectly describes how I feel when I run difficult rapids, and it is what I believe the proper mindset is in kayaking or any adventure sport. The word is "Zanshin." It is translated in many different ways, depending on the martial artist's background. The literal translation is "remaining mind" and it refers to the fluid alertness felt after an intense experience such as a martial arts bout. Originally in feudal Japan during the era of the warring states, it would not have been a bout or a sparring match, it would have been a battle to the death. The higher the stakes, the more important it is that your emotions not get in the way.

A more general and poetic translation of the meaning might be "the state of relaxed mental alertness in the face of danger." This came from describing the ideal state a samurai experienced as he was about to go into a battle where he could easily die – the feeling of being totally alert and completely relaxed.

This is not anxiety or edginess. It's a different dynamic altogether, a concept representing a different sense about the river as well as how we best face its challenges and potential dangers. In the martial arts, zanshin is assumed to come from the rigors of many years of careful physical and mental training, done with focus and discipline. The goal was not just to train the physical skills, but to train the full mental and emotional balance: facing danger without anxiety or tension, completely open and ready to act instantaneously. In some ways, this kind of seriousness of purpose contradicts what many people, particularly younger carefree paddlers, think about what they do. However, it is also a ready outgrowth of spending many years dealing with rivers at all levels, especially those paddlers pushing upward and taking on the hardest runs.

This state of relaxed alertness is in total contrast to working oneself up to fight, or "psyching" oneself up for a run. Those things are only required if something fundamental is lacking.

Running a hard river is not a battle, and it should never be thought of that way. However, it can be a very serious undertaking. I don't mean to imply that we should fight our way down the river. The emphasis of zanshin is on the character of how you approach the run. When you understand what is there and what you can do, and you have the confidence and skill, the correct mindset will appear and you are not scared. This is a much stronger and deeper level of dealing with danger. The Japanese developed it as part of their reality during the battle-scarred, feudal era in Japan, where war was a way of life and virtually all citizens took part in it, while the professional warrior class, the samurai, lived and breathed it at all times.

Physically, it is a scientific fact our reaction times are faster when we're relaxed than tense. But zanshin as applied to kayaking is far more than that, because it involves the honed skills peculiar to working with powerful, chaotic whitewater. Even moreso, it involves mental and emotional relaxation, even in the face of situations that are frightening to others. It has to be based on an accurate confidence, one built on what you know you can do, a synthesis of mind and body, of action and success.

Most people tend to think of fighting as explosive emotion, probably because we don't do much of it. But if you want an education in the highest levels of skill done with complete consequences, study how the samurai trained. Zanshin was the culmination of their great skill and composure in the face of danger and possible death. It was a perfect expression of Zen: acting with commitment without being weighed down by second thoughts, doubts, and emotional tangles. Being entirely present in each moment. This is why the samurai embraced Zen as professional warriors. I propose that a modern version of this exists in kayaking. We are not in a battle, the river is not an assassin or even our foe; but it is infinitely complex and can be deadly. You can read a line in a rapid and feel yourself into the river, but in the act of paddling you have to be prepared at every instant for the river to make powerful, sudden convulsions that you haven't anticipated. Your skill and awareness, your quick reactions and instantaneous judgment are what keep you alive and safe. Understanding the water, honing reflexes and skills, and feeling secure in your competence create the feeling you belong. You aren't nervous, you are alert and balanced. You have zanshin.

When I first found this word, I realized immediately that it was what I had been doing ever since I began running difficult whitewater. It is not a delusion, and it isn't something you can fake. It comes from one place only: an accurate reflection of what you are capable of. You must intuitively know that your capability matches what the river requires.

There are other implications. First, kayaking whitewater is indeed a martial art in certain senses, and zanshin means the same thing here as it does in swordsmanship.

Identifying zanshin in kayaking illustrates the deeper side of what we're doing, which to me is seeing ourselves flowing with one of the powers that created the world. It is a larger perspective that is humble and defined by respect, rather than being scared, fighting, or self-centeredly pouring our ego all over the river. Our sport, like all adventure sports, is a spiritual connection with nature, including her greatest powers and dangers. Treating as less than that will keep you mired in ego. And ego always creates nervousness and not zanshin.

Second, while I have been stressing danger involved with running difficult rapids, the concept applies to everybody no matter what they paddle. It is a question of having the proper mindset, built on training and confidence in what you can do, for whatever you face. Whether you are a beginner on Class I your first time out or an expert on a Class VI first descent, your ideal should be to blend with the water, pour yourself into its flow, and feel everything it is doing. Your ideal is to belong there. You may not always reach that, especially when you are beginning, but when you reach the state of zanshin, you'll know you belong.

This is a beautiful ideal of doing things out of trained balance and respect, again, because you belong there, as compared to "hucking". Dudes who are hucking drops are choosing a very different way of interacting with the water, and their purpose is more egocentric, forcing their will into the scene rather than "belonging". I saw some footage on a blog the other day where a guy – a very good young paddler – hucked a drop he obviously was terrified of. He was stuffed completely out of control, just manhandled, then rolled up at the bottom pumping his fist. Another segment showed a guy paddling off a 70-footer, landing poorly, and pumping his fists like mad when he rolled upright. That is hucking. You'd never see a samurai pumping his fist. He would be shifting his gaze and taking in the surroundings, composed and ready for the next move – illustrating "remaining mind". His mind continues to be engaged and alert, rather than overflowing with relief because he was scared and the danger is past. Look for that contrast when you watch people kayaking, and look for it in yourself. Running rapids you're scared of is the definition of poor judgment, regardless of the outcome. Hucking is the opposite of zanshin.

Lastly, it's a good idea to be more precise with our language and deeper with our philosophy. We aren't the first people to come upon danger in nature, we're only one of the latest in a long line that stretches back to the beginning of humans. Our challenges are self-imposed instead of being demanded for our survival. It would be a mark that we are using the gift of human thought to have something more than adolescent bravado describe what we do.

When I ran my hardest solos, I was steeped in zanshin most of the time despite the extreme exposure. I was in the middle of immense wilderness canyons, running hard class V+ and VI, feeling completely in tune with my environment. There were several periods where I did not reach that level, where I was faced with situations that jarred me out of it. That was a shock, but each time I quickly shifted back into that sense of flow. Finding that space is a beautiful feeling, and zanshin is the key. It is not something you can bootstrap to, but an outgrowth of who you are and how you approach the river. It is the outcome of the same long-term commitment to skill and awareness that a good martial artist has. Don't mistake it for "cool", it might look like something similar, but it isn't. Cool implies some distance, while zanshin means you are completely present and attuned to everything. It is contrary to ego. You have to remove ego from the scene because it just gets in the way. Famous Japanese swordsmen like Musashi and Tsunetomo referred to it also as "the void", probably because that described the transparency and lucidity they felt.

When something is extremely well learned, you are no longer conscious of it as a separate skill. It is merely part of you and your surroundings. That is your goal. Always work to prepare your skills, both mental and physical, and you will find something deeper and more effective than nervousness to guide you in your journey with the river.

***

The voice of the river

Once in our lives we may be lucky enough to bridge the gulf that separates us from other species, stepping through a doorway that is normally closed to find ourselves in a very different world.

Many years ago late in the summer on the Lochsa river, I had the privilege of swimming with an otter. I'd spent a long day sweating in my little diesel VW on the hot drive up from the North Fork of the Payette River. When I reached the lower Lochsa and its lush forests, I began looking longingly down into the clear, cold water. At every turn of the road the pools called to me in a low and soothing voice, until I could no longer resist.

I chose a bend away from the road where I had my privacy, and dove down into one of the deep pools. Hovering near the bottom and looking up, the sun glittered through the clear water as the current slid gracefully around granite boulders, tiny bits of mica glinted in the sunlight and trout warily lurked in the shadows below.

The water pressed cooly and quietly on my skin, welcome after the hot asphalt road and noise of the car, releasing me from the tension of the roadway and inviting me to play in the gentle current. And so I swam and caught eddies, laughing with the river until I rounded a boulder and came face to face with the otter.

He was lounging on a flat rock, soaking up the sun on a late afternoon swim and just as surprised as me. For a few seconds we contemplated each other, the otter and I, each suddenly and acutely aware that a creature from another world had joined a small, personal celebration of life. He wasn't large and was probably only a few years old, without the wizened look that age gives us all, whether we deserve it or not. Quickly his surprise seemed overcome by wonder and he raised his head with wrinkled brow, alert and tingling, but didn't move. A more skeptical person might think that he didn't startle because I didn't threaten him, but I like to think that it was because of my smile.

I floated there chest deep in the clear water, and had the distinct feeling he was looking me over, sizing me up, as one of those strange, ungainly creatures from up on the banks he had recently heard about – clumsy creatures that walked around on two legs, clambering over the rocks and splashing loudly in the river, rather than sleekly gliding through the water. I was suddenly self-conscious of my terribly unwaterlike body, evolved for walking on land and only adapted by years of learning and practice to propel me in the water. I'd been a competitive swimmer for 15 years and prided myself on my skill in the water. He was amused at my awkwardness.

His whiskers twitched and for a few moments he wore what looked like a small frown, which quickly turned to good-natured ease. In any case, I felt accepted. Without hurry, he slipped in and swam underwater, an artful expert in flow poking his head up to peer at me, here close to the boulder, and there close to the sand - not quite ready to run away and yet not quite ready to play.

We swam in the same pool for a while, each intrigued with the other but keeping a respectful distance. I knew if I watched him directly he would probably feel it a little too aggressive, so I minded my own business, with him just on the edge of my vision. He seemed unworried and probably couldn't have cared less once he had taken my measure. He swam back to his rock for a few minutes, climbed out, and shook himself to lay back on the hot rock in the warm sun, watching me, bemused at how poorly I moved in his native element. I dove down again and he was still watching when I came up. "Excuse me for bothering you," I told him politely, "but this really is a nice place and I appreciate you sharing it." I dove again, and when I came up, there was only a wet spot on the rock where he'd been. I felt a twinge of disappointment and looked around the pool and other boulders, hoping he would surface and we could continue our small conversation.

He never appeared and I couldn't tell where he went. He'd disappeared right into the water itself, as if he'd transported himself somewhere else with a mere shrug. For a moment I questioned myself and had the distinct sense that maybe I'd imagined the whole thing, but I still had the smile on my face and an image I've treasured and puzzled over ever since. He had been there, and now he was gone.

I've always wondered what I might have done to entice him to stay a bit longer, to stay and play with me in those eddies on the Lochsa river. Maybe to learn a few of the otter's words and hear what he thought about the world, to share a few memories about the Lochsa and its clear water, perhaps hearing the otter tell of all that the flowing river means and all that it hides.

It's been nearly 20 years since we last saw each other, but every time I drive by, I hear the river's voice and look down into the water to find my friend. I know he must still be there, somewhere just out of sight on one of the bends smiling at thoughts only an otter can have, at home among the boulders, fish, and sand in a way I never will be.

***

Epilogue

Rivers create some of the most beautiful and improbable landscapes on earth. Like many other people, I've been inspired by them for my entire life, and kayaking was just another vehicle for exploring them more intimately. I love the challenge, difficulty, and intensity of hard whitewater, but I also love the quiet serenity and flow of rivers.

As kayakers, we are privileged to see astonishing and difficult rivers, and follow them as they flow hidden in deep wilderness canyons. I've personally been attracted most strongly to rivers that cast an ominous shadow, like the Stikine, the Alsek, Susitna, Clarks Fork Yellowstone, and many others. If you are a seeker of truth, as I believe most kayakers are, the instant you enter these canyons the rawness grabs and shakes your core. As the dark walls climb overhead and close in around you, they shout of violence and danger. In such environments, you come face to face with who you are, as the river and seriousness demand clear answers even if you can't give them. Because of the struggle to understand why I am so enticed by such places and so drawn by the beauty of water, I've come to desire a clear expression of what it all means to me.

Flowing water operates by its own rules, and in most ways these are very different from what we deal with walking or climbing around on land. Reflexes we've inherited to keep from falling, to keep our balance, to respond to threats, all have to be turned inside out on the river. They won't work there, and we are literally cast adrift to learn new ways to live in a world that is both beautiful and very different. When somebody refers to a run as "Class VI+, the limit of controlled navigability" they probably will also add, "I'm portaging," preferring to stay with the stability of rock than the unpredictable power of a huge rapid. As kayakers, we attempt to categorize the important aspects of a river, and to some extent we succeed in relating the difficulties – but the most fascinating things are not part of our rating schemes or descriptions of rapids. We try to photograph them, to film them, and describe them in words, but they are never captured. There is magic and mystery within the water, and our raw experience opens it up to us, even if we don't have any means to capture it. They remain in our minds, coursing through our bodies in the emotions and sensations, but in the end we can't show them to others. Such are the rules – in the end you just had to be there, you had to experience it yourself.

There are instants that, for me, symbolize the magnificence of our sport. Running a big waterfall is one of those. The instant where we separate from our world into flight, we are released from the rules that normally bind us to the earth, set free to imagine something greater. Even the simple act of pushing off the bank has this feeling. The moment we're out in the water, we have set sail in a new world separated from all that is solid, and totally reliant on our skills. It's a gift of our sport that water has such a magical element to it, and our skills allow us to take part in that magic.

I remember descending deep into a gorge in Mexico where a river went underground. We were standing on a ledge in a thin veil of mist, glinting reflections of the sun off of the falling waterdrops. It was as if we were floating in the middle of a galaxy of stars, surrounded by huge double-rainbows that followed us every step. There are places so improbable and beautiful that you cannot capture them; but you can experience them and the memories live on within you.

There are rivers whose rapids require a peculiar combination of finesse and power at breakneck speeds. Virtually every rapid on the Stikine involves weathering some heavyweight roundhouses, jabs and a haymaker. You learn tricks like getting as much speed as you can, keeping your boat's angle just right and "getting small" as you plunge into the main break. When you're facing such rapids down in a deep gorge in the pouring rain, it strips you of any feeling of bravado. You put the best you have on the line, pray you can pass through safely, and then feel thankful you were able to witness one of the world's true wonders. That experience is a gift, not a feat.

And when you emerge from a canyon like that, you bow your head and give thanks for the beauty you just saw, and especially, that you are alive and able to enjoy the memories. The shared experiences with your close partners will be among the greatest of your life.

For all these kinds of experiences, there are also times I have caught myself wondering whether there is something missing. Sometimes our passion for running rivers seems like the pulse of life itself. The intense experiences, the beautiful places, the strong friendships seem to be the only answer we need. But it should be obvious that kayaking is not the sum of the world. I truly love kayaking and it has given me some of the most important experiences of my life. But if we are to have a philosophy and live by its principles, then we realize other things much more important. I've been married 25 years, have five children, a Ph.D., and I run a good-sized business serving thousands of people every year. I believe in giving back, and have been supporting a school and a number of individual children in the poorest part of Nepal for the last 15 years after an expedition there in the early 1990s. To me, as wonderful as our experiences on rivers are, whitewater is only a small part of rivers, and rivers are only a small part of a much greater world.

People who come to kayaking later in life generally have an idea of where it fits within all the other things they do. But it is easy for talented young people inspired by their love of the sport to feel it is the only thing that matters. They define their lives in terms of their paddling. If you're one of them, you are doing yourself a disservice to treat your sport single-mindedly as more important than other things you might do. Lots of younger professionals want to get paid to play. If you're good enough to do that for a while, at least ask yourself if there's something greater to live for than your fun. We live in the richest and most free society the world has ever seen; so please consider whether you have a responsibility to do something with that. Play is not the sum of life. My children and my family are who I live for – along with the other people I love. Rivers have a place, but never make the mistake of thinking that a sport is more important than the deeper responsibilities you have.

Running rivers can be anything you want to make it. You can challenge yourself, you can laugh with your friends and partners, make the river into a party, brag about your feats, joke about swimming out of a hole, enjoy the quiet, or just have the biggest smile on your face after a fantastic surf session. It's a simple fact that how you use it, and what you seek from it, reflects who you are. I've done lots of play-paddling, first descents, many expeditions, solos, and extreme descents. To me, running rivers is something much more than a feat of skill or daring.

I've chosen to make the places I go kayaking into a vision of the ideals I strive for. Certain places in this world are testaments to the wonder and magic contained in flowing water. The Grand Canyon of the Stikine is one of those, the Alsek River is another. There are many more: each a truly grand gesture of nature. I choose to be inspired by their power and beauty, to accept that I'm smaller than they are – not to consider myself greater for having done them. Neither I nor anybody else has changed these places in the smallest way by running their rapids; the only possible thing that can be changed is what's within us. In the martial arts I've practiced for much of my life, the goal is not to learn a thousand ways to kill somebody and then consider yourself better and tougher. It is to turn the challenge inward into yourself, realizing the hardest challenge is to your ego and self-understanding. The path to ego is easy and short. The path to self knowledge is difficult and has no end.

Rivers and kayaking provide both paths. It's up to you to choose which you will take.

For the past 25 years, I've pondered these and many other thoughts, and as one personal answer to an overall philosophy, I have come to treat my kayaking as a martial art. The river is the ultimate master, the master who is perfect in every movement, who can't be subdued, can't be hurt, and cannot even make a mistake. The inspiring thing is that we can learn to take part in its flow, into and through the most powerful and deadly places. The goal is to gain the skills to meet the river purely on its terms and to be humble enough to let the world be bigger than you. When you reach that stage, then kayaking is no longer a sport, and the doors are wide open to other territories. Each place we go, every paddle stroke, every river, has untold lessons to give if we seek them. The question is, can you reach into this greater arena and learn from it, finding valuable life lessons, or does it feed the lesser parts of your ego?

In the Japanese sword arts there is a theme called the "life-giving sword." The concept evolved over several centuries until it became something very different from wielding a samurai sword to kill your opponents in battle. Instead of being wielded against an outer enemy, the razor sharp edge of the sword is metaphorically turned toward the wielder himself. Instead of cutting down opponents, it is used to cut through the ego, and cut away one's flaws and weaknesses. This is a life-long journey toward an ideal and the goal is to gain a clearer understanding of ourselves. It is to create and then offer the best we have to others. The death of each old weakness gives life to new awareness: the constant birth of a new being. This is an ultimate affirmation of what it means to be alive.

To me, rivers are precisely that life-giving sword.

Whether you know it or not, at every second and in every part of your life, the sword is always in your hands.

Use it well.

***